MAN OBEYS HIS IMPRESSIONS RATHER THAN HIS REASON. IT IS NOT ENOUGH TO SHOW HIM THE TRUTH; THE IMPORTANT POINT IS TO ROUSE HIS PASSIONS FOR IT.
MIRABEAU

I OWED MORE TO THE MUSIC OF THE NATIONAL GUARD THAN I DID TO BAYONETS.
LA FAYETTE

DAVID WHITWELL

BAND MUSIC OF THE FRENCH REVOLUTION

WHITWELL BOOKS

Band Music of the French Revolution
Second edition
Dr. David Whitwell

Copyright © 2015 David Whitwell
All rights reserved.
Published in the United States of America.
All images used in this book are public domain.

Cover image: Antoine Vestier's Portrait of François Joseph Gossec with his scores for the *March lugubre* and the *Te Deum*.

ISBN-13 978-1-936512-81-2

Whitwell Publishing
Austin, TX 78701
WWW.WHITWELLPUBLISHING.COM

First edition, 1979

Second edition, 2015

Contents

Contents	8
List of Figures	9
List of Tables	11
Foreword	15
I The Participation of Bands during the French Revolution	**19**
Origins of the Revolution and the Band Tradition	21
The Music Corps of the National Guard	24
The Festival of the Federation	26
Ceremonies During the National Assembly	37
The Ceremony for Mirabeau	38
The Politicalization of Music	40
The Ceremony for Voltaire	43
The Federation, 1791	48
Band Music During the Final Days of the Monarchy	51
The Free School of Music	53
Music for the Festival of Liberty	58
Music for the Festival of Law	60
Music for the Federation, 1792	61
Band Music under the Girondins	63
The Funeral of Le Peletier	65
The Funeral of Lazowski	68

    The Federation of 1793 68
    The Funeral of Marat 69
    The Festival of Reunion 70

The Development of the Musical Institutions   75
    The National Institute of Music 75
    The Concert of November 20, 1793 78
    Musique à l'usage des fêtes nationales 81
    The Arrest of Sarrette 81

Band Music During the Terror   83
    Music for the Festival of the Worship of Reason 84
    Celebration of the Victory of Toulon 86
    Anniversary of the Death of Louis XVI 87
    Music for the Festival of the Supreme Being 88
    Music for the Celebration of Victories 94
    Music for the Fifth Anniversary of the Bastille 96
    The Celebration of August Tenth 96

Band Music After the Terror   99
    Music for the Festival of the Fifth Sans-Culottide 99
    Music in Honor of J. J. Rousseau 101
    Music for the Concert of November 7, 1794 101
    Anniversary of the Death of Louis XVI 103
    Music for the Funeral Ceremony in Honor of Feraud 103
    Music for the Festival of Liberty 104
    Music for the Celebration of August Tenth 105
    Music in Honor of the Girondins 105
    Establishment of the Conservatory 105

Band Music at the End of the Revolution   109
    Music for the décade Festivals 109
    Music for National Festivals 112
    Music for the Ceremony of Campo-Formio 113
    Music for Military Funerals 114
    Music for the Festival of Liberty and the Arts 116

II	**A Catalog of the Band Music of the French Revolution**	**117**
	Ferdinand Adrien	125
	Henri Montan Berton	126
	Matthieu Frédéric Blasius	128
	Giuseppe Cambini	130
	Charles-Simon Catel	136
	Luigi Cherubini	154
	Nicolas Dalayric	164
	François Devienne	165
	Frédéric Duvernoy	168
	André-Frédéric Eler	169
	Abbé Feray	171
	Georg Friedrich Fuchs	172
	François Réné Gebauer	176
	Michel-Joseph Gebauer	178
	François-Joseph Gossec	180
	Hyacinthe Jadin	211
	Louis-Emmanuel Jadin	214
	Rodolphe Kreutzer	219
	Honoré Langlé	220
	Xavier Lefevre	221
	Jean François Lesueur	227
	Johann Paul Schwartzendorf	233
	Étienne Méhul	235
	Étienne Ozi	242
	Niccolo Piccinni	244
	Ignaz Pleyel	246
	Henri Joseph Riegel	248
	Claude Rouget de Lisle	249
	Étienne Solère	251
	Jean Pierre Solié	252
	Johann Christoph Vogel	253

III	**Band Music for Festivals under the Restoration of the Bourbons**	**255**

The Anton Reicha *Symphony for Band*   259

The Nicholas Charles Bochsa *Requiem for Louis XVI and Marie Antoinette*   263

The Hector Berlioz *Symphony for Band*   **269**
    First Version of the Score 270
    Second Version of the Score 272
    Third Version of the Score 273
    Extant Manuscript Version of the Score 274

About the Author   277

About the Editor   281

List of Figures

1 Bernard Sarrette, photograph by Jean-Baptiste Isabey, c. 1790. 26
2 The Festival of Federation 28
3 *Fête de la Fédération* 30
4 *Antoine Vestier's Portrait of François Joseph Gossec* 35

5 Honoré-Gabriel Riquet, compte de Mirabeau, 1789 38
6 Funeral ceremony for Mirabeau 39
7 *Portrait de l'artiste* by Jacques-Louis David, 1794 42
8 Voltaire's funeral procession 44

9 *Les derniers moments de Michel Lepeletier* 66
10 *The Death of Marat*, by Jacques-Louis David, 1793 69
11 *La Fontaine de la Régénération*, by Charles Monnet, 1797 71

12 Festival of the Supreme Being, June 8, 1794 89

List of Tables

1. Copyist's note for the Catel, *Battle of Fleurus*   96
2. Copyist's note for the Catel, *Battle of Fleurus*   97
3. Copyist's note for the Méhul, *Hymn of Victories*   97
4. Copyist's note for the Gossec, *Hymn of Liberty*   100
5. Copyist's note for the Cherubini, *Hymn to the Panthéon*   100
6. Copyist's note for the concert on November 7, 1794   102
7. Copyist's note for the concert on January 21, 1795   103

I want to express my appreciation for my colleague, Craig Dabelstein of Brisbane, Australia, for his contribution to this volume. His own musicianship, broad education and skill in editing is responsible for the reappearance of this book. Any reader who places value in having this book back in print is in his debt.

Foreword

As far back in my professional life as I can remember, I have heard references to the French Revolution as being associated with the birth of the modern wind band, especially with respect to its instrumentation. Attempts to explore this subject further were frustrated by the very sparse available literature, nearly all of it in French, and the fact that only a very few compositions were available in print. Thus, while a few unpublished dissertations and articles were available, I found there were none which made critical comments, as for example sorting out the good compositions from those which were merely functional, or which identified where this music could be found today. The available sources known to me also failed to provide specific information regarding the circumstances of the actual first performances of this early band music.

On the other hand the French Revolution itself has been the subject of a vast amount of literature. At the time of this writing there were more than 1,000 publications on Napoleon alone! However, it became clear to me that in order to answer the questions mentioned above, I was going to have to go to Paris myself to do basic research. This book, then, is the product of three separate periods of work in the National Library there, beginning in the Winter of 1973–1974.

In those distant days before computers and the pressure from RISM to make their catalogs known to scholars, research was not easy. Many libraries, because of works lost in World War II, were very protective and did not welcome visiting scholars, much less make copies. It was because of the destruction caused by the war in Dresden, for example, that I was at first refused help and moreover told, "What right do you have to come look at music in our library after you destroyed it in the Dresden Fire Bombing?" Berlin, when I was there, was a special problem due to the divided city, which left the music in West Berlin but the card catalog in East Berlin. Furthermore, the old original Prussian National Library had sent out music manuscripts to small towns all over Germany in the hope that while Berlin would probably be destroyed, the smaller cities would be left alone. This was largely successful, although to this day the music has not all come back to Berlin.[1]

Some libraries would only speak to you in a single language, as Italian in Florence or French in Prague.[2] Some small libraries would not admit visitors, until continued knocking opened their doors. But many others, to be fair, were wonderful in their help.

In Paris I was quickly introduced to the publications of a man who had devoted much of his life to the study of the music of the French Revolution, Constant Pierre (1855–1918), a bassoonist and musicologist. The man collected the surviving examples of this music, including thousands of songs, and made full scores only for the purpose of then making piano arrangements from which he could study. With regard to the band music this resulted in two massive books, *Les Hymnes et Chansons de la Révolution* (Paris: Imprimerie Nationale, 1904) and *Musique des Fêtes et Cérémonies de la Révolution Française* (Paris: Imprimerie Nationale, 1899). It was immediately obvious that I had to obtain my own set of these books. This, however, was not easy. I was informed that the only remaining copies were in the basement of the Hôtel de Ville and that even the National Library could not buy an extra set, due to some ancient government rule. I visited a large number of used book stores and though they all knew these books they held no hope of my finding a set. Finally I found a small book store called *Livres du Spectacle,* owned by a cripple, who, to my astonishment, said he could get them

[1] For example, a large number of autograph scores, including many original band works, by Meyerbeer are still missing. Some libraries had sent out what they considered precious manuscripts but left the band music in the building. Thus in Darmstadt wonderful and important band works were forever lost. Not so much regretted were the loss of 100,000 marches by one of the early Dukes.

[2] When I spent some weeks in Prague it was still under the old Communist control, which resulted in a number of restrictions. I had assumed that either German or English would suffice for my work in the National Library and was thus startled when told only French would be used. I left to sit in a coffee shop for thirty minutes in order to conjure up enough French vocabulary to communicate and then returned to the library.

but it would take three days. Sure enough, three days later he had two new volumes with uncut pages and asked if $8.00 per volume were too much? Although it was necessary for me to record errors and shelf-marks which had changed over the years, the fact remains that his was a tremendous contribution which made all later books on music of the French Revolution, including this one, possible.

I SHOULD LIKE TO EXPRESS my most sincere appreciation to Heiner Schneider, of Schneider Publications, Tutzing, Germany, for kindly returning to me my copyright on this book, which makes possible this second edition.

DAVID WHITWELL
Austin, 2015

Part I

The Participation of Bands during the French Revolution

Origins of the Revolution and the Band Tradition

THE FRENCH REVOLUTION was as accidental as it was inevitable. By the end of the eighteenth century, France was the most populous nation and its capital, Paris, was the largest city in Europe. The French people were politically divided into three classes, called states or estates: the clergy, the nobility and the so-called "Third Estate." The clergy had become the rich class through the usual tithes, wills and gifts, but also by its tax exempt status. Some writers have estimated the holdings of the Church as equal to twenty percent of all the land in France! The noble class included older landed families but also a large number of those more recently made noble as the result of holding administrative positions which were endowed with nobility, in return for contributions to the King's purse.

What was the Third Estate? That question was asked and answered in a famous pamphlet published in January 1789.

> What is the Third Estate? Everything. What has it been until now? Nothing. What does it want to be? Something.

It included the poorest beggar and the richest banker, all the professions, trades, peasantry and common men.

At the head of French society was the king, Louis XVI, who became the master of France at age twenty. As absolute rulers go, Louis XVI was rather harmless and somewhat weak in character. His wife, Queen Marie Antoinette described him thus:

The king is not a coward; he possesses an abundance of passive courage, but he is overwhelmed by an awkward shyness and mistrust of himself ... He is afraid to command.[3]

In all fairness, no previous French ruler since François I could have been prepared for the problems which would face the monarchy at this time. The Queen, sister to Joseph II of Austria, was bright and full of potential. Had she been all-powerful, things might have turned out differently.

In retrospect, many scholars have emphasized the recent intellectual atmosphere as the catalyst which made the revolution possible. As the most influential views were all published a full generation before the revolution, it is perhaps more accurate to say the intellectuals prepared men for the roles they would play, rather than thrusting them into those roles. One such philosopher was the lawyer, Montesquieu (1689–1755),[4] who published his *De l'Esprit des Lois* in 1748. His views rationalized the old order as the better alternative among despotism, republican or monarchial forms of government.

Another influential writer was Jean-Jacques Rousseau (1712–1778),[5] who in his *Du Contrat Social* of 1762 called for a new concept of total sovereignty of the state. His real contribution, however, was of a more emotional nature. A contemporary said of him, "He had a great influence over the minds of the young and made madmen of people who would otherwise only have been fools."

As important as these and other philosophers were to a general climate of unrest, the real catalyst of the revolution was not ideology and the search for individual freedom, but economics and the search for food. The principle concern of the government during the years before the revolution was the search for an answer to a rapidly deteriorating state of the royal finances. One of the major contributors to the financial crisis had been the support for the American revolution, a step taken to avenge the British and one France certainly was in no position to afford. France found herself requiring about half the annual expenditure of the government for the servicing of the national debt, an expenditure which had

[3] Jeanne-Louise Campan, *Memoirs of the Private Life of Marie Antoinette* (Boston: Grolier Society, 1917), II, 216.

[4] Known by his last name, he was Charles-Louis de Secondat, Baron de La Brède et de Montesquieu.

[5] Curiously, this famous philosopher began his professional life as a music copyist, who is often quoted as saying that the way to judge a good copyist is if he can make an oboe part from a violin part. He was also a composer and some minor band marches are extant.

risen from 93 million livres in 1774 to 318 million livres in 1786. At this point the only alternative to bankruptcy was a major new source of tax funds, an idea which found support in no quarter.

The political crisis surrounding the immediate tax problem was serious enough, falling in the time of an inflating economy in general. It was pure historical bad luck that at this moment occurred one of the most catastrophic harvests in memory. Exceptionally severe hailstorms (people were reported killed by hailstones sixteen inches across) in July 1877 caused the cost of bread to double six months later. The effect of this was to make the national financial crisis immediately understood on a personal level. An English agronomist touring France in the summer of 1789 wrote that he had often heard people say that "the deficit would not have produced the revolution but in concurrence with the price of bread."

This serious and complicated political crisis emanating from the economy resulted in the king calling a meeting of the Estates General (representatives of the three classes), the first such meeting since 1614. An appeal to the public for suggestions regarding how the business of the Estates General should be conducted was taken as an end of political censorship and opened the door to the extraordinary pamphleteering which continued throughout the revolutionary years.

The local elections to select the representatives of each of the three classes resulted in polarization at the local level over numerous issues. As a result the men who met in May 1789 at Versailles were at once bitterly divided and without direction. One result was an immediate deadlock over voting procedures, which prevented the actual beginning of the Estates General for some six weeks.

In spite of the predictable maneuvering for position during this period, a genuine, even emotional sense of national opportunity was felt, particularly by members of the Third Estate. It was this body which broke the deadlock by meeting separately on June 17 under the title "National Assembly." This forced the government, which had until this point attempted to be neutral, to call a royal session, at which the king would announce his will, for June 23, as an attempt to keep things from getting out of hand.

On June 20 the Third Estate, barred from their usual meeting place because of preparations for the king's session, and fearing a possible dissolution, held an emergency meeting on a tennis court and swore never to disband until France had a constitution. This provided the first of many dramatic and newsworthy events which caught the attention and stimulated the imagination of people everywhere.

The king in his session made a number of concessions but he was only buying time, for he had already over-reacted by sending out orders for the gathering of a force of 30,000 troops, including many of foreign extraction. Now, with the atmosphere of anarchy clearly in the air, the Parisian electors decided to take over the local government and form their own militia, as protection against the "foreign" troops on one hand and potential rioters on the other. This militia, called the National Guard, was formed rapidly and was in need only of arms. It was the search for arms which led to the storming of the Bastille which gave the revolution its perfect symbol, for this famous state prison represented the past and royal despotism. Every school child in many countries still memorize that date, July 14, 1789.

From this point on, the king having completely lost his nerve, a new order existed in France. In rapid succession the National Assembly passed the reforms which remade the nation: the abolition of feudal privileges, the Declaration of the Rights of Man (Article One: "Men are born and remain free and equal in rights."), the secularization of the Church and the complete reorganization of the domestic bureaucracy.

The Music Corps of the National Guard

On the day the Bastille fell the word "band" in France meant some version of the *Harmoniemusik* of the Classical Period, but now with additional clarinets. In its smallest form, represented by a number of publications of music, it was 4 clarinets, 2 bassoons and 2 horns. If further instruments were added they tended to be flutes, perhaps a serpent, a trumpet and side drum. One does notice there seems to have been an understood limit of twelve players, an ancient association with the *Les Grands Hautbois* wind ensemble of the seventeenth century in France. The most important new characteristic was the use of the clarinet, replacing the oboe of the earlier *Harmoniemusik,* as the primary melodic instrument. It seems safe to suggest that this change was intentional, made because of the long association of the oboe as the chief melodic instrument of *Harmoniemusik,* a medium long associated with the highest aristocracy. The relatively new clarinet did not have this association and thus, in a sense, became the solo instrument of the people. And it follows that to this very day, bands have more clarinets than any other instrument.

The breakdown of the bureaucracy during the first year of the revolution has left us with few details about the bands initial involvement. The newspapers generally only documented their presence, such as on the day of the fall of the Bastille, we read of the singing of a *Te Deum* with "military music." Similar references of military music can be found in the papers for August 9, 10 and 25, 1789, although the last one still refers to a twelve-member band.

It appears that it was during the following nine months that the larger bands began to appear, perhaps if only to be heard by the ever-growing crowds of the public. There were several ceremonies in Notre-Dame designed for the blessing of the flags. In a newspaper review of the ceremony of the *Fête-Dieu* in Notre-Dame during the Fall, the presence of a larger band seems documented.

> The holy sacrament was preceded by a big part of the National Guard Music and by many drums. The sounds of this military music, mixed with the songs of the church, formed a divine concert of the highest majesty.[6]

At some point during the first year of the revolution, the band's life became associated with that of the man most responsible for the incredible repertoire described in the following pages, Bernard Sarrette. Born November 1, 1765, he

[6] *Newspaper of the Commune,* quoted in Constant Pierre, *B. Sarrette et les origines du Conservatoire National de Musique et de Déclamation* (Paris: Librarie Delalain Frères, 1895), 20.

was the son of a cobbler and lived in Paris with probably little more than a minimum education. If one can believe the comments of his later enemies, he held a minor clerical position in the Office of the Depot of the French Guards. The first official document bearing his name, after that of his birth, is a petition sent to the Assembly in June 1789. His actions at this time indicate he was already in the military and we find him again recruiting 150 soldiers from his native district, Filles-Staint-Thomas, the day before the fall of the Bastille. On the famous day itself he was part of the search for arms, supplying his men with weapons found at the Chelsea Hospital. He became a captain in the National Parisian (paid) Guard on September 1, 1789, and retired on a pension on October 9, 1791.

Figure 1: Bernard Sarrette, photograph by Jean-Baptiste Isabey, c. 1790.

We can assume that at some point between September 1789 and October 1790 Sarrette became associated with the musicians of the National Guard. As was the case with officers who had musicians in the armies of England and America, the officer in charge had to assume the personal responsibility for his musicians pay and per diem. Since Sarrette did not come from a family of wealth, as most officers did, this was certainly difficult, for his pay was only 2,800 livres.[7] He managed it by seeking funds where he could. As he reflected later, "my fortune was not considerable at that time, I didn't have anything and had no talents to earn a living. I just had good legs and good hands and I knew very well how to use them." Sarrette's success may be measured by the fact that when the City of Paris formed a central, paid music corps for the first time, in the Fall of 1790, he was selected to be chief administrator.

[7] A livre in 1789 France was the approximate equivalent of $1.25 in the United States in 1970.

The Festival of the Federation

On the anniversary of the fall of the Bastille, July 14, 1790, there occurred the first of what would become a long series of great national festivals in Paris. The popular success of this first festival caught even its planners by surprise and would immediately change the entire concept of military music in Paris. The National Assembly had chosen July 14 as a day for national celebration for obvious reasons. It sprang partly from a feeling everywhere for revolutionary solidarity and patriotic fraternity and even from a feeling that the revolution was over—that the new day was already here.

A plan was created of almost unbelievable dimensions. The site selected was the Champ de Mars, a smooth green in front of the old Ecole Militaire, where the students carried out their marching exercises and where today stands the famous Eiffel Tower. The decision was made to carve out of the earth an amphitheater capable of seating 400,000 people— an area roughly the size of ten football fields. The city hired several thousand of the poor for this labor, but both time and money ran out well before the project was finished. As a last resort the city put out a call for volunteers and an extraordinary spontaneous outpouring of the public resulted. Not only individuals of every class came, but clubs, societies in full dress, associations, Church and military units. As one participant recalled the scene,

> The great semi-circle or amphitheatre of earth ... was raised by two hundred thousand people of every age and station, both men and women ... The first step was to mark out the semi-circle, and then the level had to be raised by four feet, using the earth from the center of the arena. But that proved insufficient, so more earth was brought in from the Plain of Grenelle and from the area between the Ecole Militaire and the Invalides, where the slightly raised ground was leveled down. Thousands of barrows were pushed by people of every quality ... you would see Capuchin monks and friars pulling beside the ladies of the town, clearly recognizable by their dress ... Laundress and Knights of St. Louis worked side by side in that great gathering of all the people; there was not the slightest disorder ... Everyone was moved by the same impulse: fellowship. Everyone who owned a carriage horse sent it for a few hours every day to pull earth ... All other work was suspended, all the workshops were empty. People toiled until midnight and at daybreak were back again.[8]

[8] Felice Harcourt, trans., *Memoirs of Madame de La Tour du Pin* (London: Harvill Press, 1969), 141–142.

Food tables were set up for the workers, musicians played, and the workers themselves constantly sang "Ça ira." This famous song, born at this time was based on Ben Franklin's

Figure 2: The Festival of Federation, plate showing the triumphal arch, the ceremonial altar on the Champ de Mars and the Ecole Militaire in the background. Engraving (plate no. 39) originally published in *Collection complète des tableaux historiques de la révolution francaise.* Paris: Chez Auber, 1804.

customary answer when asked for news of his young republic, "it will be all right."

When finished, the setting was impressive indeed. There were seats for 400,000 and three huge triumphal arches, adorned with allegorical figures, through which the procession would pass. There was a special pavilion for the king and his attendants, covered with striped tent cloth of the national colors and decorated with streamers and *fleurs de lys*. In the center, on a base twenty-five feet high, was a temple of flowers and greens and *L'Autel de la Patrie* (Altar of the Fatherland) with incense burning, and room for two hundred priests.

Governmental and military representatives from all parts of France began making their way to Paris for the event. They were called *fédérés* (those who band together, confederates) and from them the ceremony would take its name. These people were feted in each town they passed and of course the object of more celebration in Paris itself. This very spontaneous part of the atmosphere carried over into the planned events as well.

On the great day a procession began at the site of the Bastille, at 7:00 in the morning[9] consisting of the National Assembly, the Parisian Guard, representatives of the army, the federates from throughout the country, a battalion of boys (armed like their fathers), a body of old men (as in ancient Sparta), and of course bands, floating banners, patriotic inscriptions, costumes and flowers everywhere. The procession moved across the city, past the Tuileries, past the Place de Ferronnerie where Henry IV was assassinated (here there were tears of emotion) and, amidst a volley of artillery, and across a bridge of boats which had been thrown across the Seine the previous day. Through the triumphal arches they went, eight abreast, into the amphitheater.

The ceremony began with a Mass officiated by Talleyrand, at this time Bishop of Autun. This sinister figure was among the few persons who participated in a hypocritical frame of mind. As he passed Lafayette at one point it was reported he said, "Don't make me laugh."[10] Perhaps, therefore, it was fitting that during Tallyrand's portion of the ceremony intermittent rains soaked the assembled. After the Mass, Talleyrand blessed the Oriflamme of Saint-Denis[11] and the eighty-three banners of the departments.

A profound silence fell on the Champ de Mars as Lafayette, appointed that day as commander in chief of all the nation's armies, advanced as the first person to take the civic oath to the new Constitution. As he moved toward the altar, trumpets sounded and then the vast military band began to play until he ascended the steps.[12] He placed the blade of his sword, given to him by George Washington, on a bible on the altar, raising his other hand toward the sky, and pronounced: "We swear to be forever faithful to the Nation, to the Law and to the king, to maintain to the utmost of our power, the Constitution decreed by the National Assembly and accepted by the king." As if by command, at this moment the sun at last broke through the clouds, creating a rainbow over the enormous arena as thousands of brass buttons shone! Lafayette, now at the very height of his popularity, was caught up in a maelstrom of public enthusiasm.

[9] F. A. Mignet, *History of the French Revolution* (London: George Bell & Sons, 1896), 88.

[10] Maurice de La Fuye, *The Apostle of Liberty* (New York: Thomas Yoseloff, 1956), 135.

[11] A banner first used by Louis VI in 1124 and last flown in the battle at Agincourt in 1415. A version of it remained in the Abbey of St. Denis.

[12] *Memoirs of General La Fayette* (Hartford: Barber & Robinson, 1825), 252.

He was surrounded by people who covered his coat-tails, his boots, his stirrups and even his horse with kisses.

Next the members of the National Assembly took the same oath, each in his own name, each followed by shouts of "Vive la Nation!" Now the most tension-filled moment came as it was the king's turn. In view of the dramatic version of the oath taken by Lafayette, Louis XVI decided that it would be a mistake to drag his fat and flabby body up to the altar. Since he also considered the oath to be little more than enforced perjury, he merely stood under his canopy, pointing his hand toward the altar, and muttered the oath. The ceremony concluded with the first performance of Gossec's *Te Deum*, w. 79,[13] composed for the occasion. It should be noted that there were similar ceremonies coordinated to occur throughout the nation at precisely the same time. An eye witness reported that a *Te Deum* was also sung in the cathedral in Rheims.[14]

[13] The "W" identification numbers refer to the revolutionary band repertoire found in Part 2 of this book.

[14] Letter of C. B. Wollaston (July 18, 1790) quoted in J. M. Thompson, ed., *English Witnesses of the French Revolution* (Oxford: Basil Blackwell, 1938), 83

Figure 3: The *Fête de la Fédération*, Champ de Mars, in July 14, 1790.

After the ceremony ended in Paris there followed for days fireworks, balls and sporting events all as part of the celebrations of July 14. One touching sight was a public dance held on the ruins of the Bastille itself, with a hand-made sign reading, "Place for dancing." A contemporary noted, "They danced indeed with joy and security on the ground where so many tears had been shed; where courage, genius and innocence had so often groaned, where so often the cries of despair had been uttered in death."[15]

Like the ceremony itself, the *Te Deum* by Gossec represented the end of something and at the same time the beginning of something. It would be the last abstract choral work, and the last in Latin, for several years. At the same time its very success would create a new form and tradition. In selecting Gossec to compose this first "national" music the authorities were clearly turning to a member of the establishment, a dependable and respect composer, who at age fifty-six was at the peak of his profession. Holding this stature, he would compose more revolutionary wind music than anyone else, indeed so much so that the younger composers would later complain.[16]

In deciding to compose a *Te Deum* for the ceremony, Gossec was following examples of recent memory, for as we have mentioned above there were in the past year several instances of the combination of military bands with music of a sacred nature, including two previous Te Deums. However, as the word spread of this part of the preparation for the ceremony, letters began to appear in the public papers expressing a strong sentiment against the appropriateness of a *Te Deum* for this occasion. Following a suggestion in favor of a *Te Deum* made by a painter named François,[17] an anonymous correspondent wrote to the editors of the *Chronique de Paris* on June 24, 1790:

> I am sure at that moment canons will roar, the flags of liberty will be raised and a forest of sabers will appear, which is all good and I am sure tears will come to my eyes ..., but what will I have to say to the Eternal? Full of the feelings of liberty and the enthusiasm it inspires, do you think I will be content to cry *Te Deum*? And in the first place, why sing in Latin at a French celebration?
>
> The *Te Deum*! ... one sung that for the birth of Charles IX, for the birth of Louis XIV; it is the song of crimes of childishness, certainly what was appropriate for that would not be

[15] Quoted in Mignet, *History of the French Revolution*, 89.

[16] *Affiches de la commune*, August 31, 1792.

[17] *Le Journal de la Municipalité*, June 6, 1790.

appropriate on July 14. The *Te Deum*? One sings that when one fights, often when one is beaten, when one is bad, when one ravages the countryside, killing millions of poor devils who were created only to kill or be killed—Oh! that is not a hymn for July 14 ...

I demand a French hymn, something above a *Te Deum* ... Let the execution be simple! Let young men who are not twisted and young girls as naive as liberty sing the hymn to the God of Liberty. The refrain will be repeated by the choir of 24 million men.

On July 9, a citizen calling himself "The Child of Liberty" wrote the same paper, associating himself with the position of the above letter.

All zealous patriots, and there exist many others, applaud the letter which you have included in your paper. A people reborn, a people who celebrate the conquest of liberty must speak a new language. No longer the *Te Deum,* the abuse one has made of this song does not allow us to sing it on so august a celebration as July 14. We must have another.

Nevertheless, Gossec, who must have been aware of the discussion in the press, chose to compose a *Te Deum,* no doubt because of the intended sacred character of this ceremony. The composition must also have been influenced by the plans to have it performed by massed forces. One official account said the performance was done with 300 drums, 300 wind instruments and 50 serpents.[18] The newspaper, *Moniteur,* for July 23, 1790, reported there were 1,200 musicians to the right of the altar.

Here we must acknowledge Gossec's remarkable achievement, for no one in past history had ever been required to compose for such vast numbers of musicians, or music to be heard in such a huge outdoor public arena. He very wisely chose to have all these wind players take the role of an organ with much of the *Te Deum* text sung in unison, in the style of chant. The result is a very effective work, simple but very noble. The modern listener will be surprised to find also, among the movements of the *Te Deum,* two secular dances, very lively instrumental works. There appearance here no

[18] *Details de la fête nationale du 14 juillet 1790 arrêtés par le roi* (National Archives, document AD VIII, 16).

doubt follows in the tradition of the Baroque French Ballets and the English Masques, where separate instrumental works were performed when time was needed for a change of scenery, or for the actors to reposition themselves.

The autograph score calls for a band of fourteen wind instruments, consisting of pairs of small flutes, oboes, clarinets in C, trumpets, horns, alto winds (probably tenor oboes or some substitute), bassoons with a single percussion instrument, the *tonnerre* ("thunder"). A later hand has added "et serpent" to the bassoons staff and has written "timballes" to obscure the name, "tonnerre." Since the small flutes only double the oboes, we recognize here the twelve-member band size which had long been associated with the French court, beginning with the *Les Grands Hautbois* of François I.[19] The "tonnerre" was a very large bass drum with which Gossec was acquainted with from his work in the Opera. An extant document, signed by Gossec, testifies to this.

> I certify that Mrssrs. Huard and Joly, machinistes of the Opera were employed to transport the large drum, called le tonnerre de l'Opera for use with the music of the Federation on July 14, 1790.[20]

The impact of this performance of Gossec's music had far reaching repercussions. First, while it is a familiar tradition known to the modern reader that music can have a powerful impact on large outdoor audiences, including sporting events and political rallies, the leaders of this great ceremony were taken quite by surprise by the effect of the music on the public. They assumed the focal point would be the events taking place on the altar, but for those 400,000 attending who could probably hear nothing being said on the altar, it was the music which was the highpoint. From this point on the government leaders became increasingly concerned with using music as a political tool, to influence the thinking of the population. Thus immediately in 1790 we find a recommendation by Devienne,

> The people need songs, celebrations, spectacles. When one wishes to interest the people whose imagination is alive, and

[19] It is this long wind band tradition which explains Mozart's choice of 12 winds for his *Gran Partita*, K. 361.

[20] La Bibliothèque de Nantes, Nr. 22208.

whose spirits are not too enlightened, it is to the senses one much speak.[21]

[21] Quoted in Constant Pierre, *Les Hymnes et Chansons de la Révolution* (Paris: Imprimerie Nationale, 1904), 2.

Second, the success of the military bands themselves, due to their contribution to the success of this first great festival, convinced the government that the permanent support of a central military band was opportune. By October 1, 1790, the Commune of the City of Paris had established a paid music corps of the Guard, renting a residence at the cost of 3,000 livres and establishing three levels of rank with corresponding pay of 330, 450 and 540 livres.

For the conservative members of society there was a negative reaction to this great ceremony and its music, as General Bouillé complained, "that fête poisoned the spirit of the troops." Indeed, the festival with its tumultuous reception for the regulars and the National Guard, did spread revolutionary sentiment among the troops. But discipline had already begun to break down during 1790, in part due to the desertion of many of the (noble) officers who left the country in fear of the new society. The most serious immediate development was the "Nancy Affair," of August 1, 1790. A garrison of troops in Nancy, provoked by a punishment, mutinied. Bouillé, sent by Lafayette to resolve the situation, overreacted and in the process 500 were killed. Some thirty-two of the culprits were hanged and forty-one condemned to the galleys. All were members of the Swiss regiment of Châteauvieux.

This instance of French killing French, coming so soon after the euphoria of the Festival of July 14, captured the attention of the public. In response the city of Paris organized a memorial funeral service for the victims of the affair of Nancy, which was held on the Champ de Mars on September 20, 1790. One of the two band compositions performed at this ceremony was a transcription of the *Overture to Demophon*, w. 158, by Johann Vogel. While this band transcription is apparently lost, an early French dictionary reported that it was performed by 1,200 wind instruments with "unparalleled success." The most important original band work performed at this ceremony was the *March lugubre*, w. 73, by

Gossec, a work we can date by a portrait of Gossec by Vestier. In the picture a notebook of music, placed on a table, reads "Marche lugubre for the funeral honors which must be rendered by the Champ de la Federation, 20. Sept. 1790 for the citizens who died in the affair at Nancy," followed by the first measures of the score.

Figure 4: *Antoine Vestier's Portrait of François Joseph Gossec* with his scores for the *March lugubre* and the *Te Deum*.

This is an extraordinary composition in every way, not the least of which is a level of inspiration and emotion rarely found in Gossec. Contrary to all tradition of the march form, this march is fragmented, interspersed with haunting silences which are usually filled by the ominous sound of the gong—an instrument never before heard in France before this composition. Strange and dramatic harmonic moments add both great mystery and power to the work. It is one of Gossec's best efforts and was often performed. Few compositions at this time inspired so much comment from the listeners. Of this first performance the *Journal de la Municipalité* of September 23, 1790 wrote,

> The sharp noise of the tam tam (instrument arabe) combined with cymbals and brass and interrupted by intervals of silence gives to the soul the most sorrowful sensations and inspires a contemplative mood.

A performance of this work in April, 1791, for the funeral of Mirabeau brought similar reactions by the listeners. The *Révolutions de Paris* wrote that "the notes, detached from one another, break the heart, pulling at ones insides," while the *Moniteur*, of Aprl 6, 1791, found "the mournful roll of the drum and the sound of the funeral instruments filled the soul with religious terror." Mme. de Genlis, who heard this performance, commented on the "prodigious effect" of the silences which "produced shivers, the veritable silence of the tomb."[22] Further evidence of the impact of this march can be found in the fact that these features, the gong and the silences, can be found in many later band compositions, for example in the *Funeral March* which opens the Bochsa *Requiem for Louis XVI* of 1815.[23]

[22] Quoted in Pierre, *Les Hymnes*, 842.

[23] Further performances of this march can be documented in the following Revolutionary ceremonies entitled The Festival of Law and The Federation, both of 1792. In a procession of 1793 for the Funeral of Lazowski several bands performed this march and Gossec himself conducted a work for chorus and band at the grave side ceremony.

Ceremonies During the National Assembly

September 1790 – September 1791

THE NEW CONSTITUTION which it was hoped would hold the nation together during the period of rebuilding did not have an opportunity to really be tested as a form of government. This Constitution of 1791 called for an elective legislature, but with an executive appointed by the king. The object of the constituent National Assembly at this point was neither democracy nor true social revolution, but rather a more open society in which talent and not just birth would count. However, social pressures on all sides prevented the stable atmosphere needed for *any* new form of government to be fairly tested.

The sale of Church property did not lead to a new pattern of land ownership. Since the point of the sale was to raise funds, it had the effect of only reinforcing the previous pattern of wealth. Although the emphasis was now a rivalry between the very rich and the very poor, the old divisions of the three orders would remain clearly discernible for some time.

All the noble had actually lost was the formal recognition of his qualitative distinction from the rest of the population, but these pretensions were very real and deeply held. The number of nobles who emigrated continued to grow and by 1791 half of the army officers had resigned.

The strongest contributor toward the failure of the new constitution was the King. His own background made it impossible to accept the role given him in the new order of things, much less see it as the best option he would ever have. The King and Queen played for time, still believing a true general revolution among the lower classes would restore things to the former status quo. Even as he took the oath to defend the constitution, in September 1791 thus formally accepting it, his wife was writing the Austrian ambassador, "giving the impression of adopting the new ideas is the safest way of quickly defeating them."

One of the ways the king expected to temporize was through the relatively open practice of bribing influential nobles and citizens for support and it was in this manner that the loyalty of Mirabeau[24] (1749–1791) was acquired. In return for the king's paying some of his substantial debts, Mirabeau worked on a policy to save the monarchy which entailed separating the king from the rest of the nobility.

[24] Honoré Gabriel Riquet, comte de Mirabeau.

On January 4, 1791, the Assembly chose Mirabeau as its president. To general surprise he proved a very hard working and impartial leader. Unfortunately he also drank hard and played hard. On the evening of March 25 he entertained two dancers from the Opera and the following morning complained of violent intestinal cramps, leading some to suppose he had been poisoned. After a period of suffering, he died on April 2.

Figure 5: Honoré-Gabriel Riquet, compte de Mirabeau, 1789

The Ceremony for Mirabeau

ON APRIL 3, THE ASSEMBLY decided to convert the Church of St.-Geneviève into a shrine for French heroes and to be called the Panthéon, "of all the gods." Because of his recent office and untimely death, great public interest existed in Mirabeau and he was the first to be placed there.[25] The ceremony consisted of an extensive funeral procession held on April 4, 1791. Representatives of the departments, municipalities, popular societies and the Assembly marched together with some 20,000 of the National Guards from Chaussee d'Auntin to the Panthéon in an unbroken procession.[26] An estimated 400,000 people watched from the streets, from

[25] On August 10, 1792, evidence that Mirabeau was being secretly paid by the king was discovered and the following month the Convention ordered his remains removed from the Panthéon.

[26] Louis Barthou, *Mirabeau* (London: William Heinemann, 1913), 308.

balconies, trees and roofs. The body was carried by twelve sergeants of the regiment to which Mirabeau belonged. The procession passed in mournful silence, broken only by the rolling of drums and funeral marches. One historian thought it was "the most extensive and popular funeral procession that had ever been in the world."²⁷

²⁷ Jules Michelet, *French Revolution*, I, 568.

Figure 6: Funeral ceremony for Mirabeau

The only march which can be identified by name as having been performed on this occasion was the Gossec *March lugubre,* w. 73. As mentioned before, this march made a profound impression on its listeners. The *Révolutions de Paris,* April 1791, found "the notes, detached from one another, break the heart, pulling at ones insides." In the same style the *Moniteur*, April 6, 1791, wrote "the mournful roll of the drum and the sound of the funeral instruments filled the soul with religious terror." Mme. de Genlis, an observer commented on the "prodigious effect" of the silences which "produced shivers, the veritable silence of the tomb."[28]

[28] Quoted in Pierre, *Les Hymnes*, 842.

The Politicalization of Music

WITH THE CEREMONY for the transfer of the remains of Voltaire to the Panthéon, the wind band music of the Revolution enters an entirely new phase. For the next few years the ceremonies, including the use of music, would be carefully staged efforts at mass political indoctrination. What were the roots of this philosophy?

The use of music to inculcate religious dogma or civic duty is as old as the ancient Hebrews, Greeks and Romans, as the later French Revolutionists would often point out. More recent examples were constantly available in the Church. As the *Journal des hommes libres* pointed out,

> If the Credo sung from infancy inured so many men to believe what they did, why should Truth not seize the means which error has employed with such success?[29]

[29] Quoted in James A. Leith, *Media and Revolution* (Canadian Broadcasting Corporation, 1968), 54.

French intellectuals had prepared the way for some time. Montesquieu in *L'Espirit des Lois*[30] commented on the belief of the Greeks regarding the influence of music in the state, as did Voltaire.[31]

[30] Montesquieu, *L'Espirit des Lois* (Geneva: Barrillot, 1794), IV, viii, ii 87.

[31] *Oeuvres complètes*, ed. Moland (Paris: Garnier, 1877), II, 544–545; III, 373.

Rosseau, who had maintained that the arts were demoralizing, nevertheless stressed the political and social utility of festivals.

> What! Must there be no spectacles in a Republic? On the contrary, there must be many. It is in the Republic that they are born, it is in its bosom that one sees them sparkle, with a veritable air of fête ...
>
> It is in the open air, it is beneath the sky that you must assemble and give yourself up to the sweet sentiment of your happiness ... But what will be the objects of these spectacles? What will one demonstrate there? Anything if one wishes.[32]

[32] *Oeuvres complètes*, ed. Musset-Pathay (Paris: Dupont, 1824), II, 175–176.

With a strong native philosophical background, together with the fact that three-quarters of the French population was illiterate (including many nobles), the leaders of the Revolution could not help but seize the opportunity to use music to build support for their political aims. Mirabeau had pointed out,

> Man obeys his impressions rather than his reason. It is not enough to show him the truth; the important point is to rouse his passions for it.[33]

[33] Quoted in David Dowd, *Pageant-Master of the Republic* (Lincoln: University of Nebraska, 1848), 83.

A provision for national festivals was actually written into the Constitution of 1791 by unanimous vote. In one form or another the government and the various political parties would henceforth use the festival as a means of mass communication. By 1794 the government would outline an entire master plan for national festivals. These would include major ceremonies celebrating each year the Fall of the Bastille, the overthrow of the monarch, the execution of Louis XVI, etc. Lesser ceremonies would honor the Deity, Nature, Martyrs of Liberty, Love of Fatherland, Agriculture, and Youth Old Age and Marriage. Every tenth day all year would be set aside for a festival.

As a result of the success of the first festivals, revolutionary music would also be heard in the theater and in scores of vaudevilles, operas and ballets. Thousands of songs were written intended for the individual to sing. An editor of a collection intended for soldiers, for example, hoped that before the battle the soldier would sing revolutionary songs instead of praying. Still another collection was intended for the home, to be sung with guests. Another body of revolutionary songs was intended for the primary school. These included not only hymns, but songs designed to teach civic duties and obligations. One writer even prepared for children a versified version of the 1793 *Declaration of the Rights of Man*.[34] More recently such songs were heard in China under Mao, who was a scholar of earlier revolutions.

[34] Leith, *Media and Revolution*, 56.

Did it work? Apparently so, for testimonials are easily found such as the one by Duboucet, made before the Convention in 1794.

Nothing is more appropriate than patriotic hymns and songs to electrify the souls of Republicans. When on mission in the departments I was witness to the prodigious effect which they produce. We used always to end the meetings of official bodies and of the popular societies in singing hymns, and the enthusiasm of the members and spectators followed as an inevitable consequence.[35]

[35] *Moniteur,* January 16, 1794.

Another review from the same period reads,

We are brought then to the conclusion that there is nothing more important than national festivals. For they furnish us with the best means to confer social virtues upon a whole people, and to preserve them; to establish and purify the national customs; to give birth to and to reinforce for them that powerful, active and fruitful enthusiasm for the laws of the Fatherland, liberty, equality and for all the principles which lay the foundation for the common honor and for the happiness of all.[36]

[36] Thiébault, quoted in Dowd, *Pageant-Maker,* 127.

Certainly one factor in the success of the festivals was the participation of Jacques-Louis David, the foremost French painter of his generation. He was attracted to the Revolution as an opportunity to free art from the prejudices of the old regime and to return to the idealized concepts of Greece and Rome. As he became more and more involved with the festivals, while art like music became more and more a tool of the state, the direction was more in trying to find a visual expression for the new concepts of *liberté, fraternité* and *patrie.* David's influence as an organizer and artist with impact and utility led naturally to his becoming a politician. In 1792 he was elected deputy of Paris to the Convention and would eventually become honorary President. His most important role was as the influential member of the Committee of Public Instruction, a post from which he would in time dominate the planning of the festivals.

Figure 7: *Portrait de l'artiste* by Jacques-Louis David, 1794

The Ceremony for Voltaire

WHEN VOLTAIRE DIED IN MAY 1778, the Archbishop of Paris refused him Christian burial, so his friends quickly interred him at Scellières before the Bishop of Troyes could object. After church property was nationalized in 1789, his old friends began to campaign for his return to Paris. In reaction to the Papal denunciation of the Civil Constitution of the Clergy in April 1791 the Assembly voted in favor of an elaborate ceremony to glorify Voltaire.

In addition to this strong anti-Church character associated with the ceremony, there was an anti-monarchy sentiment which was even stronger. This came about as a result of the royal family's decision on June 20, 1791, to try to escape from Paris, an attempt which failed near the frontier where they were recognized by peasants. While some called for dethronement, the Assembly feared such move at this time might spark a foreign war, thus they announced that the king had been "kidnapped." This had the result of provoking a storm of radical opinion in Paris, where the truth was known, led partly by the working class, whom were now becoming known as *sans-culottes*, because they did not wear the knee breeches of the nobility.

The ceremony was originally set for July 4, but various delays, including heavy rain on the 10th and morning of the 11th postponed the event until the afternoon of July 11. Great numbers turned out when the coffin reached the capital on July 10. It was brought into the city on the shoulders of eminent men, with Lafayette riding in front on horseback as far as the site where the former Bastille had stood, a place where Voltaire had twice been held captive. The coffin was placed between lighted candelabra and the population filed past in an unending column.[37]

The procession left the Bastille in mid-afternoon on the 11th in a carefully organized parade with the theme, "to emulate the pomp and grandeur of the Greek apotheoses and the Roman consecrations." Paraphernalia, costumes and even

[37] Anadreas Latzko, *Layfayete* (New York: the Literary Guild, 1936), 210.

Figure 8: Voltaire's funeral procession

new musical instruments had been constructed after sketches by David, who while studying in Rome had carefully copied figures from the Trajan column and from museums. The focal point was a great triumphal wagon, designed by David, towering above the rest of the procession and bearing the sacred remains. It was drawn by twelve white horses and led by attendants in Roman costume.

As in the Mirabeau procession, representatives of all levels of government were included, together with representatives of schools and theaters. The procession included banners with suitable mottos, a model of the Bastille, pictorial representations of Rousseau, Mirabeau and even Benjamin Franklin. Just before the triumphal wagon a figure of Voltaire, dressed in a gown, was carried sitting in an elbow chair. On the wagon itself was the coffin and arranged above it, in a bed, another waxen figure was laid out.

Two eye-witnesses left us a colorful, first-hand reports of how this all looked.

> The whole was got up in theatrical style. All the actors and actresses, singers and dancers of the different theatres were grouped around a statue of the philosopher, in the various

costumes of his *dramatis personae*. Zaire was walking next to Mahomet, Julius Caesar arm-in-arm with Oedipus and Brutus with the widow of Malabar; while another group represented Calas and his family. One of the most singular objects in the procession was a portable press, which worked off various handbills as the *cortège* proceeded, which were scattered amongst the people.[38]

...

I cannot, however, praise the triumphal wagon; as a machine *à l'antique* it was incorrectly conceived, as a piece of modern production it was heavy and clumsy. The horses, 12 in number, were beautiful in the extreme ... The figure of Voltaire lying upon its back on the wagon produced but a sorry effect, especially when, on account of the unevenness of the pavement, it could not be kept steady; the right arm too was dislocated by the repeated jolting of the carriage and hung down like the arm of a malefactor broken upon the wheel. The show, nevertheless, gave universal satisfaction and did not arrive at the cloister, where the body was to be interred, until after 9:00 at night; I say the body, but more properly what was left of the body.[39]

[38] J. G. Milligen, quoted in Thompson, *English Witnesses*, 134.

[39] Stephan Weston, quoted in Thompson, *English Witnesses*, 135.

The procession made various stops (in obvious imitation of the Stations of the Cross in Church processions) throughout the city, including the *Opéra,* the *Comédie Italienne,* the *Comédie Française* and at the home of the Marquis de Villette. He was married to Voltaire's sister and it was there Voltaire died. At this place we know the band and singers performed the Gossec *Patriotic Chorus*, w. 83. An unscheduled stop was made at the Tuileries beneath the windows of the royal prisoners. As night began to fall the rain began again, but on they went lighted by the torches of David's art students. At about 9:30 PM they arrived at the *Panthéon* where the sarcophagus was installed next to that of Mirabeau.

Contemporary accounts indicate vast crowds watched all this, in numbers which compared with the ceremony for Mirabeau. The reaction probably varied between those who saw it as a deeply moving spectacle and those who saw it as a grotesque farce—depending on one's political perspective. The pro-revolutionary press of course praised the ceremony. The *Chronique de Paris*, for example, called it "the most beautiful and most imposing of festivals."

Adverse observations were made primarily by members of the nobility. Madame de Genlis called it "the most foolish, abominable and ridiculous absurdity that was ever seen in Paris prior to the festival of Reason."[40] Another who watched was Lord Palmerston of England, who remembered,

> It was very long, but a great part of it consisted of very shabby, ill-dressed people whose appearance was made worse by the mud and dirt they had collected. Great quantities of the National Guards attended; but in disorder and without arms.[41]

Two band compositions, both by Gossec, received their first performance as part of this ceremony. One, the *Hymn*, w. 82, has survived only in the form of a song for solo voice, accompanied by clarinets, horns and bassoons. Constant Pierre was confident it was used in the ceremony because he discovered more than sixty manuscript parts for the band accompaniment.

The *Patriotic Chorus*, w. 83, is of particular interest due to the appearance of two "new" instruments in the French band. In the autograph score they are called *"petites et grandes trompes antique,"* but they soon became known as the buccin and tuba curva. It is clear that they were actually used in the procession, for at least one newspaper already knew the names and commented on the sound they uttered.

> We think we owe to those interested in the progress of the arts a note on the instruments antiques which were used under the direction of M. Sarrette, through who's zeal and intelligence the funeral of Voltaire was made so interesting. The largest are those which the ancients called cornua curva—they gave the sound of six serpents. The smallest are called buccins—they have the sound of four demi-cors.[42]

Sarrette himself recalled the invention of these instruments in a speech given on November 20, 1793, during intermission of a concert given for the members of the government.

> The composers, who are accustomed to producing music for the theaters and concert halls, noticed that they did not have

[40] Quoted in Dowd, *Pageant-Master*, 52.

[41] Quoted in Thompson, *English Witnesses*, 133.

[42] *Chronique de Paris* (July 14, 1791), quoted in Walter Dudley, *Orchestration in the Musique d'Harmonie of the French Revolution,* unpublished dissertation, Berkeley, 1969, 122.

the same results in open air when the same instrumentation was used. They searched for a solution. From the ancient Greeks they reconstructed the tuba curva and from the Jews, the buccin. The tuba curva was part of the ornaments of the ancient coach of Voltaire. Its given shape and dimensions were calculated by the composers and the sound which was needed was produced very successfully. The second instrument, the buccin, produces an absolutely new and terrible sound. We can hear this instrument at a quarter of a lieue away. There are only three notes possible, but a construction allows the musicians to change pitch.[43]

As Sarrette was speaking in support of his Institute in that speech, we may doubt if the introduction of these instruments occurred in a process so thoughtful. Likewise, the explanation given by Dudley that the idea was taken from specific earlier instrumentation books seems an improbable idea.[44] The present writer prefers to assume that the whole idea originated with David. He probably took the sketches he had made in Rome of similar instruments on the Trajan column and had someone make such instruments.

It is very difficult, in the absence of sufficient surviving specimens, to know just what these instruments were. These names appear and disappear across the centuries never meaning quite the same thing. Probably they were both a variant of the large French-style hunting horn, but without the completed circle. Constant Pierre examined, in 1893, an instrument for sale described as a *"trompe de chasse."* He was able to trace the Parisian maker to a man who died in 1794. Thus he concluded this was in fact one of the original instruments used in the Voltaire ceremony,[45] and as it turned out, this instrument produced only the fundamental, octave and fifth used in the part. At the turn of the century this instrument was included in the Museum of the Conservatoire.

[43] Quoted in Dudley, *Orchestration*, 111–112. A *lieue* is about 2½ English miles.

[44] Ibid., 117ff.

[45] Pierre, *Les Hymnes*, 212–214.

The Federation, 1791

THE SECOND ANNIVERSARY of the fall of the Bastille was again celebrated with a ceremony called The Federation. It was not as elaborate as in 1790, with no triumphal arch, no bridge and procession over the Seine, etc., but it was still an event of some size as we can see in a rather lengthy account by Lord Palmerston.

> The great altar, which is a building raised high from the ground to which four ample flights of steps in a circular form lead up, on which altogether I doubt not but 2,000 persons might stand, was in the middle. The Ecole militaire, a very handsome building, is at one end; the other extends nearly to the Seine. The whole area except in front of the Ecole militaire is surrounded by a bank of a breadth and size proportionable to the place, sloping inwards down to the area, on which last year there were benches placed. This year the people stood. The numbers it would contain cannot be estimated. The people of Paris were pouring out to it the whole morning and yet it was not half full, though at a little distance it appeared to the eye of a spectator tolerably well covered. The troops which consisted of a large detachment of the Gardes Nationales of Paris and all the neighborhood I should suppose might amount to 20,000 ... the procession consisted besides of great bodies of troops which marched with them, of detachments from all the great bodies of people concerned in all the departments of the government, the Courts of Justice, the Academies and various Societies of the Capital. The National Assembly who last year attended in a body sent this year a deputation of 24 members. The whole procession marched to the altar where were already placed about 60 priests, all in their white robes of ceremony, and as candles could not be used four fires were kept burning at the corners in vases raised on vast tripods in antique forms. The whole altar was now a cluster of people; and the banners which every Corps carried before them formed a circle completely around it. The Mass attended with musick took up some considerable time and afterwards the banners were carried in procession round the altar for a great while and every one in its turn was presented and had a long ribbon with the national colors tied to it. This closed the business.[46]

[46] Quoted in Thompson, *English Witnesses*, 135–136.

The "musick" referred to was a repetition of the Gossec *Te Deum*, w. 79, performed in 1790. One distinct difference with the 1790 ceremony was the absence of the king. Cheered in 1790, he was in 1791 a prisoner with virtually no support among the populace. This was stressed in a review of the ceremony in the newspaper, *Bouche de Fer,* of July 15, 1791.

> The name of King was effaced from the tablets of the Altar. Nearly 300,000 men successively inundated the Champ de Mars; following on in crowds, like a torrent, a sea, an ant-hill of men; and thousands of voices cried, "Live free and without the King!"[47]

The feeling of unity and national celebration was not nearly so strong, as compared to 1790. This, and perhaps the efforts which had gone into the Voltaire ceremony just three days earlier, may help account for the lack of enthusiasm exhibited by the establishment. This attitude can be seen in the diary of the American Ambassador in Paris, who treats the ceremony as something barely worth mentioning.

> Thursday 14. This Morning shortly after Breakfast I walk out and call on Mr. Franklin, who is abroad. Then on to Mr. Le Cuteulx who is also abroad. Sit a little while with his Wife, then go to the Champ de Mars where there a great Multitude assembled to celebrate by a Mass the Anniversary of the Capture of the Bastille. After walking about here a while and feeling the Approach of Fatigue I return. On my way examine the Operation of a Water Screw which is more considerable than I expected.[48]

Besides the performance of the *Te Deum*, there was a performance of the *Hymn for July 14*, w. 81. This hymn was advertised once under the title "written for the Federation of 1792." However, we do know it was performed at the Federation of 1791, for it is quoted in a newspaper, *Trompette du père Duchesne* (July 20), in its review of the ceremony.[49]

The band made at least one additional appearance in July, on the 30th, which is known only from mention in the newspaper, *Moniteur,* as a ceremony "for the maintenance of the voluntary soldiers who went to the frontiers."

[47] Quoted in A. Aulard, *The French Revolution* (New York: Russel & Russel, 1965), I, 299.

[48] Gouverneur Morris, *A Diary of the French Revolution* (Boston: Houghton Mifflin, 1939), 217.

[49] Quoted in Pierre, *Les Hymnes,* 203.

The king, because of his greatly weakened political position, finally signed in September the document which made the Constitution official. For the celebrations attendant upon this event the band made its final appearances during this phase of the Revolution. In Paris, in a ceremony to celebrate the signing held on the Champ de Mars, the band performed the Gossec *Patriotic Chorus*, w. 83. This performance included some of the best professional singers in town, those of the choruses of the Opera, Theater Feydeau and the Royal Chapel.

In a similar ceremony in provincial Strasbourg the *Hymn of Liberty*, w. 153, by Pleyel for band and chorus was performed. The poet, Rouget de Lisle, later recalled the occasion:

> It was performed in the open air at the *Place d'Armes*, performed by a colossal orchestra conducted by Pleyel himself. The musicians first played a strophe, then it was repeated by the immense populace which filled the square to its limits and to which was attached the military bands of all the numerous regiments attached to the garrison.[50]

[50] Quoted in Pierre, *Les Hymnes*, 218.

Band Music During the Final Days of the Monarchy

October 1791 – August 1792

The final year of the monarchy saw an increasing breakdown in authority and leadership on all sides, resulting in a headlong rush toward that moment in French history known as "The Terror."

The election for the new Legislative Assembly was held amidst furious activity by the journalists; Paris alone in 1790 having 133 journals. Most political leaders had their personal journals as a platform for public influence. Napoleon would later blame the fall of the monarchy itself on its failure to participate in this journalistic battle.

Another source of competition for leadership was the "clubs," political parties of sorts, but not in the modern disciplined sense. These clubs formed the base of the power struggles in the new Assembly, particularly since the old Assembly had stipulated that all of its members should be ineligible for membership in the new one. The "Feuillants" sat on the right side of the hall, conservative and supportive of the monarchy. On the left, on an elevated platform, were the Girondins, sometimes called "the mountain." In the center, "the plain," were a large group who claimed to be unaffiliated. One influential group was called the Jacobins and it had numerous affiliated clubs in the provinces. As time went on each of these factions attacked more and more ferociously the others, each believing all their opponents to be betraying the ideals of 1789.

Those nobles who had emigrated at the beginning of the Revolution had by this time begun to have demonstrative success in gathering troops abroad and gaining the help of other monarchs with the aim of a restoration. The king and queen of France during this period were covertly supporting this as an all or nothing tactic. The result was that on April 20, 1792, the Assembly declared war on Prussia and Austria; war would be a factor in French politics until the final defeat of Napoleon twenty-three years later.

In early summer the Assembly sent out a request to the departments for representatives to attend the third anniversary of the fall of the Bastille. The representatives from Marseilles sang, as they marched through France, a new song called "Hymn of War," but which would soon and forever be named after those who sang it, "The Marseillaise." The origin of this song began at a dinner in the home of the mayor of Marseilles for civil and military leaders. Those assembled agreed that it was a pity that the nation had no song to stir the hearts of men. They invited Rouget de Lisle, a local poet and musician, to compose such a work. He returned home and immediately composed both words and music. On the very same day the mayor called his guests back to dinner, to receive "an important communication." Everyone was curious what this was, but the mayor said nothing throughout the dinner. When the dinner was finished, the mayor suddenly sprang up and without introduction sang, in a vibrant tenor voice, the hymn!

As it turned out, the representatives from Marseille arrived too late for the ceremony in question but stayed on in Paris due to the obvious atmosphere of an imminent crisis. This atmosphere worsened considerably on July 28 with the announcement on behalf of their majesties of Austria and Prussia of an ultimatum. One part of that ultimatum gave the city of Paris, and the Assembly, a clear choice of restoration or invasion. On the next day a leading member of the Jacobin club, Robespierre, called for the immediate overthrow of the monarchy and the establishment of a republic. On July 30 the representatives from Marseilles took up the cry.

In the following days section after section of the city notified the Assembly that it no longer recognized a king. On August 9, Marat published an appeal for the public to rise up and arrest the king and his family and on August 10 a mob of some nine thousand did exactly that. In the process they killed hundreds of the king's Swiss guards, slaughtered the household staff, sacked the palace, set fire to numerous buildings and arrested the royal family. Some of the civilians made banners from the red uniforms of the dead Swiss guards—henceforth the red flag would be associated with revolutions.[51]

[51] Georges Sorel, *Reflections on Violence* (New York: Huebsch), 194.

The Free School of Music

ON OCTOBER 13 THE GUARD BAND performed the Gossec *Patriotic Chorus*, w. 83, and a now lost Gossec setting of a text by Rousseau at a celebration of the acceptance of the constitution. The event was sponsored by a Calvinist club, with the mayor being present. So it was a bitter surprise that on the next day the band members saw the publication of the order for the new organization of the National guards which contained no provision for the support of the band.

Foreseeing that they must move immediately to establish a need for themselves which would serve as the foundation for the financial support of the band itself, they had a memorandum presented to the town council on October 17 calling for the establishment of a conservatory, a "military music academy" to train troops of the line. A strong statement of support was added by the *Chronique de Paris*.

> The music of the National Guard deserves to be distinguished for the influence it has had over the Revolution. We would refuse to see what is obvious if we contested this influence and we wouldn't know the consequence of this powerful art if we had not believed that the sums of money for its progress were well used. If we weren't certain of the fact, we would just notice the impressive words of La Fayette who repeated several times that he owed more to the music of the National Guard than he did to bayonets. These musicians have, in

fact, participated in all the public ceremonies and in many of the actions of the Revolution. Gossec can therefore be called the Musician of the Revolution, seconded by Sarrette with a zeal which is above all praise. There are now, among the instrumentalists of this music corps, some artists of superior talent and a great nation ... should be ... conscious of their cost.[52]

[52] Quoted in Pierre, *B. Sarrette*, 23–24.

Further support came from Charles Villette, the nephew to Voltaire, who recalled their contribution to the ceremony of July 11, adding,

> We need the zeal of that brave citizen, Sarrette, who gathered the musicians. We should encourage the establishment of a military music academy ... The sons of the National Guard would receive free music lessons. In three or four years we could hear five or six hundred young citizens singing with their teachers, and together they could set up civic concerts which would be worthy of the best days of Athens and would attract attention from all of Europe.[53]

[53] Quoted in Pierre, ibid., 24–25.

The town council agreed to consider the proposal. Sarrette, apparently in an effort to hurry a decision, attempted to resign and requested his pension. In a further bureaucratic response the council "misplaced" his application for two years.

The members of the band had no choice but to continue to function without pay, in hope of an imminent decision by the council which would create a permanent basis for their existence. The band performed in two major festivals, described below, and in addition gave a public concert in January 1792 at the Lycée des Arts. This concert consisted primarily of chamber music, including a trio for clarinet, horn and bassoon by Gossec, but concluded with some of Gossec's works for band and chorus, probably w. 81, w. 82 or w. 83. A review of the concert by the *Chronique de Paris*, January 23, 1792, concluded,

> The merit of this performance can be evaluated easily when we think that the men who participated were probably the most talented wind instrument performers in Europe. We profit from that circumstance and pay homage to the zeal that

the music of the National Guard showed during the public fêtes, and we ask the National Assembly to establish a more expansive institution which this great empire deserves.[54]

[54] Quoted in Pierre, ibid., 25–26.

Finally on June 8, 1792, the General Council prepared the order for the creation of a free music school of the Parisian National Guard.

> According to their offer, the music corps agrees to train one hundred and twenty pupils of the sixty battalions, the sons of the citizens serving in the National Guard, between ten and sixteen years of age for those who have not received any musical training, and between eight and twenty years of age for those who are already musicians.
>
> I
>
> When the pupils arrive ... they will be tested by the Major to determine the kind of instrument in which they will major.
>
> II
>
> The pupils will receive two courses of solfeggio weekly, each lasting one hour, they will receive one hour each week in the course of study in their instrument and when ready will be admitted to the general rehearsals.
>
> III
>
> The schedule shall contain study hours.
>
> IV
>
> Students will take their lessons only at the time indicated, except if they are changed for an extraordinary service.
>
> V
>
> The pupils will perform with their teachers in the National and public fêtes.
>
> VI
>
> The pupil will be responsible for the complete uniform, instrument and music paper.
>
> VII
>
> A copy class will be established in which the pupils, after their lessons, shall be held for an hour to copy the music necessary for their studies.

VIII

Students who escape from the established discipline will be suspended from school for eight days, two weeks, or a month, depending on the gravity of the offence. In the case of repeated fault they may be dismissed according to the decision made by a committee composed of the Commandant, five teachers and four students.

IX

There will be an annual public concert in the presence of the Municipal Corps.

X

Finally, it is essential that every pupil admitted possess the physical qualities necessary for their profession, specially for wind instruments.[55]

[55] I am indebted to David Swanzy for providing a copy of this historic document for me.

Many of the original documents of this period were burned, making it impossible today to establish the original faculty. We do know that the original forty-five members of the Guard had increased to seventy-eight in 1790, and then reduced to fifty-four in 1792 due to the incorporation of some of these men into bands which accompanied troops in the newly declared war. As for the School, the earliest document which has survived listing the personnel is an extensive payroll memorandum dated November, 1793. It gives, in addition to the interesting information regarding relative pay, the instrumentation available for appearances.

Captain, Major: 3500 livres
Bernard Sarrette

Lieutenant, Music Master: 2500 livres
François Gossec

Music Master, assistant: 1500 livres
Jean Xavier Lefèvre, clarinetist

Music Sergeants: 1400 livres
Michel-Joseph Vinit, nicknamed Vény, entered January 1, 1792, Secretary

Sergeants: 110 livres
Antoine Buch, horn
Thomas Delcambre, bassoon, entered on January 1, 1792

François Devienne, flute, died on September 6, 1803.

Corporals: 1001 livres
Jean Meric, clarinet
François Simonet, bassoon until 1798
Philippe Widerkehr, trombone, entered September 1, 1789

Teachers, First Class: 850 livres
Ernest Assman, timpani, clarinet, solfeggio, administrator in 1794
Ignace Blasius, bassoon
Brielle, replaced by Cherubini on June 19, 1794
Simon Catel, composer, solfeggio, harmony, entered January 1, 1792
Andre Chelard, solfeggio, clarinet, from April 1 1790 to November 21, 1795; re-entered February 20, 1800
Frederic Duvernoy, horn, entered Aril 1, 1790
Georges Fuchs, clarinet, solfeggio
André Gallet
Joseh Garnier, until March, 1797
Matthias Gerber, clarinet
François Guthmann, trumpet, solfeggio
Charles Hervaux, horn
Antoine Hugot, flute, died September 8, 1803
Joseph Kenn, horn
Louis Lefèvre, clarinet, re-enterd in 1824
Gabriel Leroux, solfeggio
Jean Mathieu, serpent
Etienne Ozi, bassoon
Jacques Pagniez, solfeggio, manager in 1794
Jacques Schneitzhoeffer, flute, oboe, entered January 1, 1792
Guilaume Schwent, horn, solfeggio
Henry Simrock, horn, solfeggio
Etienne Solère, clarinet
Georges Stiglitz, died September-October, 1796
Louis Tulon, bassoon, dead on March 5, 1799
Othon Vandenbroeck, horn, solfeggio
Nicolas Vaucheler, trumpet
Gaspard Veillard, serpent, bassoon, entered October 1, 1793, dismissed in 1794,
    re-entered as teacher of solfeggio in 1795

Teachers, Second Class: 700 livres
Ferdinand Adrien, solfeggio
Pierre Delcambre
Michel Gebauer, oboe in 1792
Etienne Horace, entered in 1792, died in 1799
Claude Jerome
Marie Laloie
Antoine Layer, clarinet

Arnald Le Gendre, clarinet and solfeggio
Jean Paillard, horn
Louis Voisin, larine until July, 1796

Teachers, Third Class: 600 livres
Pierre Angée
Gabriel Hardouin, trumpet
Felix Miolan, oboe
François Paocher
Nicolas Rochetin
Marie Sarazin, bassoon
Frédéric Schreuder
Jean-Marie Hostie, died May 13, 1794[56]

[56] Quoted in Pierre, ibid., 36–37.

Music for the Festival of Liberty

THE OFFICIAL, but very controversial, Festival of Liberty was largely a personification of some of the increasingly polarized political views during the final months of the monarchy. The focus of the Festival and the debates were the surviving Swiss soldiers of Châteauvieux of the "Nancy Affair," discussed above. At that time, August 1790, these soldiers were considered traitors. Now, in one of those strange reversals of history, a number of people were beginning to think of them as heroes, for having refused to return the fire of the French soldiers sent to end the mutiny. Specifically, the question was: do these soldiers, now serving aboard a French galley ship, deserve to be covered by a general amnesty of September 30, 1792? The Jacobins championed the cause through pamphlets, articles, speeches and even two plays, *Les Suisses du Château Vieux* and *La Marche de Bouille*. For them the Nancy Affair was thought of as a counter-revolutionary plot. The mayor, Pétion, supported the idea of the festival because he sensed the popular support for it. The Department of the Seine, however, was against it as was the Feuillant and counter-revolutionary press. This group continued to call the Swiss public enemies.

For two weeks an intense battle of words continued, but in the end the Assembly voted honors, by a narrow margin, for the Swiss on April 9 clearing the way for the festival. On April 11 the released galley-slaves reached Versailles where the local Jacobins entertained them in the now famous tennis court.[57] Then they were presented to the Assembly, in Paris, with great fanfare.

The festival was held on April 15, which being a Sunday allowed the populace to turn out in great numbers. In fact the bulk of the participants were the common people of Paris, those from the poorer sections. The radical popular societies were out *en masse*, as well as students, large numbers of the National Guard and veterans. The theme was that the freed Swiss represented the emancipation of humanity from the shackles of tyranny.

In the parade were the usual flags (even one of the United States), busts of great men, antique sarcophagi (dedicated to the Swiss and National Guard who died in the Nancy Affair) and a model galley. The center piece was again a huge triumphal wagon constructed by David. Using the wheels and platform from the Voltaire ceremony, it now carried a statue of Liberty, adorned with patriotic bas-reliefs, and pulled this time by twenty-four brewery horses. The forty surviving Swiss marched preceded by forty virgins carrying their chains. Bringing up the rear of the parade was a jester, representing those who had tried to prevent the ceremony.

The parade, which began in late morning, required most of the day for its passage through town, stopping for singing by the crowd, a stop at the mayor's palace and a stop at the statue of Louis XV—where the figure was blindfolded and given a red hat. By evening they reached the Champ de Mars for the actual ceremony. Here on the Altar of the Fatherland another statue of Liberty now stood. Flags and emblems were laid before the statue and there was a ritual ceremony.

As far as we can determine, the participation of the band of the National Guard was limited to a performance, in front of the Opera, of two new, and not particularly inspired, works by Gossec, the *Chorus of Liberty*, w. 84 and the *National Round*, w. 85. Because this ceremony did not have the support of all officials the entire band apparently did not ap-

[57] H. Morse Stephens, *A History of the French Revolution* (New York: Scribner's, 1891), II, 61.

pear, but rather a large segment of volunteers. In any case, the appearance of the band on this occasion would later pose a problem to be explained by Sarrette.

As can be expected, the press favorable to the left found great praise for the event. The press of the constitutionalists, such as the *Journal de la cour et de la ville*, called it scandalous and ridiculous. The *Journal générale de France* wrote, "Nothing could be as shabby or as miserable as this ... noisy ... mob ... of the very poorest inhabitants."

Music for the Festival of Law

CONSIDERING THE APPARENT CELEBRATION of mutineers in the ceremony just described, it is easy to understand how the stage was now set for a counter-festival. The Constitutional Monarchists seized upon the death of Jacques Simonneau, the mayor of Estampes, who had been killed by rioting peasants over the price of grain on March 3, as the occasion for a Festival of Law. The planners appealed to the Assembly to make it a national festival demonstrating that it was "time to prove that the inflexible reign of law had finally come." But for the public it failed to create excitement as it seemed clearly only a royalist exercise.

The procession included a bas-relief depicting the death of Simonneau and performances of the *March*, w. 73, by the National Guard Band. When the procession reached the Champ de Mars it took on a decidedly militaristic flavor. Here the band performed a new and rather vigorous work by Gossec, the hymn, *Triumph of the Law*, w. 87, and perhaps another work now lost, a funeral *Hymn*, w. 86. One account says that prior to the performance of the first hymn it began to rain. Thereupon the band began playing an unscheduled "Ça ira," causing the crowd to ignore the rain and begin dancing. When the rain stopped, the religious atmosphere re-established itself with the performance of the Gossec work.

Again the press which was politically aligned with the planners, such as the *Mercure universel*, found the ceremony, "a most imposing spectacle." Those opposed, such as the *Révolutions de Paris,* found "this jumble of antique religious ceremonies and modern military evolutions resembles nothing so much as a rehearsal for the Corpus Christi procession." David, who was of course excluded from the preparations for this ceremony because of his involvement with the preceding one, found it to be the "hodgepodge of bizarre and grotesque costumes, which a Visigoth of the twelfth century would not have had the bad taste to put together."[58]

[58] Reviews quoted in Dowd, *Pageant-Master,* 72.

Music for the Federation, 1792

A GREAT TRAGIC AIR hung over the annual celebration of the fall of the Bastille held in 1792. Indeed just three days before the Assembly had declared "the Fatherland is in danger." Even the Champ de Mars seemed to have been transformed into an armed camp. No longer were there the magnificent altar, nor priests, but instead tents everywhere: eighty-three for the departments, one for the Assembly and king and another for administrative bodies.

The centerpiece of these ceremony was a huge tree, the tree of feudalism, rising from a vast pile of crowns, tiaras, cardinal's hats, St. Peter's keys, ermine mantles, doctor's caps, titles of nobility, coats of arms, etc., which the king was to ignite.[59]

The procession, going first to the site of the Bastille, arrived at the Champ de Mars at about noon. This procession of Federalists, National Guard and troops of the line was carrying a printing press as once before for the instant printing and distribution of materials, in addition to the usual banners and models of the Bastille. As these thousands of persons, together with a sea of observers, attempted at once to enter the field a great scene of disorder naturally occurred. At this moment also, the king, making his first appearance at this event since 1790, came out from the military school where he had been waiting. Only by the greatest exertions could the Guard escort the king through the mob to the altar, where he was to

[59] Louis Thiers, *The History of the French Revolution* (Philadelphia: J. B. Lippincott, 1894), 277.

once again be forced to take the oath to the constitution. An eye-witness described this moment:

> The expression on the queen's face will never be blotted from my memory. Her eyes were red from crying ... My eyes followed in the distance the king's powdered hair amid all those dark-haired (unpowdered) heads, his coat, embroidered as in times past, contrasted with the clothes of the populace that was pressing around him. When he ascended the steps to the altar, it was as if a holy victim were offering himself voluntarily to be sacrificed ... From that day, the people did not see him again except on the scaffold.[60]

During this ceremony the band and chorus performed once again the *Hymn for July 14*, w. 81, and in addition a new work, the *Hymn to Liberty*, w. 88, both by Gossec.

After the king was deposed on August 10, there was a ceremony on August 26 in the Tuilleries, the national garden, for the citizens who died in that historic event. Newspapers mention the performance of the band in the Gossec *March*, w. 73, and an additional work which cannot be identified today but which one paper called "a powerful music."[61]

[60] Madame de Staël, quoted in J. Christopher Herold, *Mistress to an Age* (New York: Bobbs-Merrill, 1958), 114.

[61] Pierre, *B. Sarrette*, 30.

Band Music under the Girondins

August 1792 – August 1793

ALTHOUGH WE ARE NOT YET in the period known as "The Terror," the overthrow of the king on August 10 signaled an end to the period of compromise and equivocation and the beginning of a period which could not help but be chaos. The fire was fanned in part by a series of rapid military reversals during which the Prussians gave every appearance of reaching Paris itself in the near future. The Parisian authorities quickly put up melodramatic posters to help recruiting which read, "To arms, citizens! The enemy is at our gates." In this atmosphere a rumor was spread that a plan was afoot to release all political prisoners and convicts in a counter-revolutionary bid for power.

At this point, the *sans-culottes* took arms, as the posters suggested, and began a month of butchery. Prisons were emptied of any Swiss, any priest, monarchists or ex-servants of the king or queen. Informal judgment was passed on them and they were murdered in the streets, more than 1,200 in the first few days of September alone. The scene is inconceivable. Princess de Lamballe, a friend of the queen, was beheaded, mutilated and her heart eaten on the spot by a fervent republican, and then her head placed on a pike outside the queen's prison window. So it went.

The elections were held in late September for the new Assembly, now called the Convention. It was a carefully managed election, with nearly 6.3 million of 7 million eligible voters staying away from the polls. The Girondins were able to achieve an uneasy control, with the leading opposition now being the Montagnard, those called "the moutain." An extraordinary, if temporary, turn of events at Valmy on September 20 placed the French armies in control of the frontier again, giving a period of somewhat relaxed tension under which the Convention could operate. During this Fall the Convention officially declared the First French Republic.

One great devisive issue remaining was the fate of the king. Any fair trial would involve the possibility of acquittal, so nothing more than a pretense was ever considered in that direction. On January 17, 1793, a majority voted for his death, and so it happened four days later. It was a day, one spectator later recalled, when "everyone walked slowly and we hardly dared to look at one another."[62]

During the Spring of 1793 problems mounted giving the enemies of the Girondins every opportunity to suggest that the government was not equal to the challenge. There was further inflation, food riots, revolutions in the chief provincial towns, including Lyons, Marseilles, Caen, Toulon, etc., and virtual civil war on the western front with military setbacks.

As a result the new constitution was set aside and a dictatorship for twelve set up, called the Committee of Public Safety. Robespierre now began to believe that only a strong Montagnard government could save the republic. Since he could not personally risk leading an overthrow he was forced to play a game of "wait-and-see" while encouraging the *sans-coulettes* to take action. The political scene become so complex by the end of May 1793 that historians even today are not confident what exactly happened. The end result was a popular resurrection in Paris on May 31–June 2 which ended with the arrest of twenty-two leading Girondin deputies. This cleared the way for Robespierre, who would in all but dress rule as a monarch and for the Terror.

[62] Quoted in Jean Robiquet, *Daily Life in the French Revolution* (New York, 1965), 9.

The Funeral of Le Peletier

THE GUARD BAND continued in the Fall of 1792 and Winter of 1793 performing the usual functional duties common to all bands. We know of their appearance at a gathering on September 22 to celebrate the proclamation of the Republic, when the Gossec *Hymn,* w. 83, was performed, and again on October 14 to celebrate the French Armies of Savoy. The really unusual ceremonies of this period, however, were three great funerals in early 1793, for Le Peletier, Lazowski and Marat. These ceremonies were a virtual canonization of Republican Saints.

On the night before the execution of Louis XVI a distinguished deputy, a Jacobin who had voted for the death of the king, was himself murdered by a former royal bodyguard. Believing themselves threatened with possible violence, his colleagues decided to form their protection by arousing public opinion against any remaining royalists and in the process turning their fellow regicide, Le Peletier, into a "Martyr of Liberty." This was done by pronouncements to the public ("It is not against the life of a deputy that the blow has been dealt but against the life of the nation.") and by calling upon David to organize a great public funeral which would underline the tactic.

Marie-Joseph Chénier, the poet for many of Gossec's hymns, made the report to the Convention regarding the funeral preparations. He clearly set the tone as one of a political, and especially non-religious, ceremony.

> Let superstition make way for the religion of Liberty ...
> All eyes shall look upon the body of our virtuous colleague and see the fatal wound it received for the cause of nations ... the blood-stained garments of the victim shall strike our citizens with horror ... The genius of a David will give life to this feeble sketch, whilst Gossec will lead the strains of that lugubrious but touching harmony that marks a triumphant death.[63]

[63] Quoted in the *Journal des Débats et des Décrets,* January 22, 1793.

Following this report, the Convention voted to attend the ceremony in a body.

The funeral ceremony began on January 24 at the home of Le Peletier's brother on the Place des Piques. A platform was erected upon which were placed a black foundation, studded with tears of silver, upon which was the actual bed upon which the victim had died. Upon its bloodstained sheets was placed the body, stripped to the waist, displaying the gaping wound on the left side all clotted with blood and with the arm hanging out. By the side of the body lay the victim's clothes and the murderer's blade, besmeared with fresh blood. David had taken up a position nearby where the crowd could watch him paint this scene, on a canvas now lost. All this occurred during the morning to the accompaniment of a chorus singing plaintive songs and the muffled roll of drums.

At 12:30 the Convention following the National Guard, marched to the site. The President mounted the platform and placed a crown of oak-leaves upon the dead man's brow. More speeches followed. While the body was being prepared for the procession to follow, a chorus of a thousand voices sang a *Hymn to the Divinity*[64] by Gossec. We have for this procession a complete roster, which may be representative of many of them.

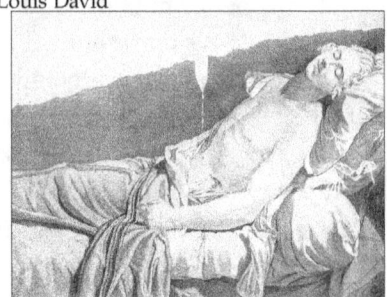

Figure 9: *Les derniers moments de Michel Lepeletier*, an engraving by Anatole Desvoge after the painting by Jacques-Louis David

[64] This title is given in Edmond Biré, *The Diary of a Citizen of Paris during the Terror* (London: Chatto & Windus, 1896), I, 303. No composition under this title has survived.

> A detachment of gendarmerie, headed by trumpeters
> A body of sappers
> Artillerymen without their guns
> A squad of twenty drummers with muffled drums
> The banner of the Declaration of the Rights of Man
> Volunteers from the 6 legions of the National Guard and 24 standards
> Muffled drums
> A banner inscribed with the Convention's Decree concerning the burial of Le Peletier in the PanthÃl'on
> Pupils from the national schools
> The Commissioners of Police
> (A great variety of civic officials)
> The figure of Liberty, borne by citizens
> Muffled drums
> The fasces of the 84 departments
> The Provisional Executive Council
> A detachment of the Convention Guard

The clothes of Le Peletier, all dripping blood
The members of the Convention, in 2 columns
Le Peletier's body on its bed of state, borne by citizens. A bladder filled with blood was placed in the gaping wound and at each jolt a few drops of blood spurted out, rousing the fury of the mob.
A band of artillerymen, with drawn swords
The band of the National Guard
Le Peletier's family
A group of mothers leading their children
A detachment of the Convention Guard
Muffled drums
Armed federates
The Jacobin Club and other societies
Cavalry and trumpeters

Following this, of course, was the public. The procession as usual made a number of stops: before the *Palais de l'Egalité*, the Oratory, at Pont Neuf, the Hall of the Friends of the Rights of Man, at the crossing of the *Rue de la Liberté* and at *Place Saint-Michel*; at most stops speeches were given.

At 4:00 the procession reached the Panthéon, where the confusion was tremendous due to the prior arrival of the public. Inside another speech, by the President of the Convention, followed by several scenes of bad taste, the victim's brother throwing himself on the body and a member of the crowd grabbing the sword and swinging it around. The ceremony concluded with the performance of a *Hymn* by Gossec, text by Chénier, which was described as a "mournful chorus sung by 1,000 voices."[65] This hymn was probably the lost one used for the funeral of Simonneau, w. 86.

[65] Pierre, *B. Sarrette*, 31.

Three days later the band participated in a ceremony during which a tree, the "Oak of Brotherhood," was planted. This ceremony was used by the police who suddenly closed in trapping numerous spies, royalist agents and deserters.

The Funeral of Lazowski

THE SECOND "REVOLUTIONARY SAINT" was one Claude Lazowski, a rather insignificant figure known in Paris mostly for his brawling and who died from drink and debauchery.[66] Because he had figured in the events of August 10, Robespierre decided to use him for another public anti-royalist demonstration. Robespierre declared him to be "un grand homme" saying, "for the past two days have I wept over Lazowski and my whole soul is plunged into grief at the immense loss."

Again the procession was organized by David and it occurred on April 28. The procession began at the *Hôtel de Ville*, the city hall in Paris, and concluded at the *Place de la Reunion*, where Lazowski had supposedly given the signal to begin the attack on the Tuileries on the tenth of August. Banners were carried ranging from "Let those who love me follow me" to "He was always a friend of the poor." The procession was made up of the usual civic officials, political clubs, artillery regiments, the regiment of which Lazowski was a member carrying his coffin. A bed of state was also carried upon which the victim's daughter sat. A number of bands performed Gossec's funeral *Marche lugubre*, w. 73, and the composer himself conducted the chorus and band at the grave-side ceremony.[67]

[66] Biré, *Diary of a Citizen*, II, 61.

[67] *Révolutions de Paris*, XVI, 266.

The Federation of 1793

The *Chronique de Paris* published on July 4 the order of the procession which would go from the Convention to the Champ de Mars for the traditional celebration of the fall of the Bastille.

> A detachment of cavalry
> Drummers
> A detachment of infantry
> The Statue o Liberty, draped with the national colors and borne by men clad in ancient Greek costume

Representatives of each section, the municipality and the
   Assembly
A bundle of pikes, bound in red, white and blue, bearing
   the words, "City of Paris"
A group of women preceded with a banner which read,
   "Young women, be fruitful for the happiness of your
   children is assured."
A copy of the Constitution in the arms of a statue of
   Minerva
Old men holding children by the hand, with the banner,
   "Happy Children, enjoy the benefits of the
   Constitution."
Bands of music
A group of people showing their joy by dancing
The *Conseil-Général*, with a stand holding the minutes of
   the votes of the sections for the Constitution
A detachment of cavalry

The ceremony began at the Convention Hall. The *Moniteur* for July 17 tells us that the band played two symphonies, a three-voice *Hymn*, w. 81, followed by a "large chorus." Unfortunately, only one of these works can be identified today.

The Funeral of Marat

THE MURDER OF MARAT in July 1793 so captured the minds of the public, that Robespierre found himself in the position of trying to play down the funeral ceremony. He was as jealous of Marat in death as he was in life.

The day before the funeral, Marat's body with its gaping wound, together with his bathtub and inkstand, was exhibited to a large crowd in the Church of the Cordeliers. The procession was held at night, beginning at 7:00 PM. The bier was borne by twelve men, escorted by girls dressed in white and by a group of boys carrying cypress branches. Next came the bath and inkstand, followed by the usual civic leaders and political clubs.

At midnight the procession reached the burial place on the grounds of the Grey Friars Club. Here a tomb had been

Figure 10: *The Death of Marat*, by Jacques-Louis David, 1793

constructed with Marat's heart in an urn above the door. Speeches and music followed.

The Festival of Reunion

In early summer the new republic was at one of its lowest ebbs. Military events were going badly, there were civil revolts throughout the country and even in Paris itself, food shortages were still a problem and the developing lack of confidence in the Girondins made the political situation very unsettled. Thus it was that the Convention decided a demonstration of national solidarity was needed to restore unity and confidence. The approaching anniversary of the overthrow of the monarchy on August 10 provided an ideal occasion. David was put in charge and given a budget of more than a million livres for the ceremony!

David wanted the procession to begin at 4:00 in the morning in order that the sunrise itself would be part of the ceremony—representing the illumination of Truth. The procession consisted of all the usual popular societies with their banners and the members of the Convention who carried an official copy of the constitution in an ark. The one unusual aspect of the procession was a large group of people whom, to emphasize the "unity" theme, were purposely indiscriminately massed together. David's plans for this group were as follows:

> Thus one shall see the president of the provisional executive council abreast with the blacksmith; the mayor with his scarf side by side with the wood-chopper or mason; the judge, in his robes and his plumed hat, next to the dyer or shoemaker. The black African, differing only in color, shall walk beside the white European. The interesting scholars of the institution for the blind, drawn on a moving platform shall present the touching spectacle of misfortune honored. You, too, shall be there, tender nurslings of the foundling asylum, carried in white bassinettes. You shall begin to enjoy your civil rights which you have so justly recovered. And you, worthy laborers, you shall carry in triumph the useful and honorable tools of your calling. Finally, in the midst of this numerous and

industrious family, one will especially notice a truly triumphal wagon formed by a simple plough on which well be seated an old man and his aged wife, pulled by their own children—a touching example of filial devotion and veneration of old age.[68]

The military was represented by a triumphal chariot drawn by eight white horses and containing an urn in which had been deposited the ashes of heroes who had died for their country. This was surrounded not with the usual marks of mourning, black trim, or muffled drums, but by the relatives of the heroes who bore garlands of bright colored flowers and a band which played music of an enlivened nature.

The procession made five official stops as it crossed town, the first being at the site of the Bastille. Here a Fountain of Regeneration in the form of a colossal statue of Nature had been constructed. Around its base were the words, "We are all Nature's children" and from two ample breasts spurted forth jets of water into a vast ornamental basin—an emblem of nature's fecundity. The President of the Convention, Hérault-Séchelles, took a superb agate goblet, filled it from a breast and said,

[68] Quoted in Leith, *Media and Revolution*, 68.

Figure 11: *La Fontaine de la Régénération*, by Charles Monnet, 1797

O Nature, Sovereign both of savage man and of civilized nations! This immense people gathered together before your image at the first ray of the dawn is worthy of thee—it is free. O Nature! may the expression of the eternal attachment of Frenchmen to thy laws be acceptable to thee, and may this beneficent water which gushes from thy breasts, may this pure beverage with which our first parents quenched their thirst, consecrate in this cup of Fraternity and Equality the oaths which France will take on this, the fairest day that has ever dawned.[69]

The President drank from the cup and then, with a flourish of trumpets, passed it on to the eldest of each of the eighty-seven deputations from the primary assemblies. The first of these elders said as he raised the cup, "I am on the verge of the tomb, but I think I shall be born anew with the regenerated human race."

The second stop was a great triumphal arch on the Boulevard Poissonnère commemorating a march of the public on Versailles early in the revolution. Around the base were words such as, "The people's justice is terrible!" and "But its mercy is great!" On the sides were paintings of the heads of the massacred body-guard at Versailles and under the arch, seated on guns, were heroines of the march carrying olive branches. Here the President exclaimed,

> What a glorious sight is this! Here we have the weakness of women allied to heroism! O Liberty! these are thy miracles! ... O women! Liberty attacked by a host of tyrants has need of a whole nation of heroes—it is your duty to produce them! Instead of the flowers which adorn beauty, the representatives of the sovereign people offer you these laurels, which are an emblem of courage and victory for you to hand down to your children.

Next the procession halted at the Place de la Révolution where formerly a statue of Louis XV had stood. Now on the same pedestal stood a plaster figure of Liberty surrounded by young oak trees decorated with tributes to the goddess. At the base a pile of wood was arranged upon which were ornaments of the monarchy: a model throne, crown, scepter, escutcheons, arms, etc. The President said,

[69] This and following quotations are from an observer, Biré, *Diary of a Citizen*, 41ff. He, by the way, was reserved in his reaction, I am not one of those who are enthusiasts about this festival, but it would be childish not to admit that as a whole it was grand and imposing ... The Republic, however, is still a hateful thing to me, and the water which flows from the breasts of the statue of Nature will not wash out the blood with which it is stained.

Here it was that the blade of law struck down the Tyrant. Let them be also destroyed, these shameful insignia of a slavery which despots have sought to perpetuate in every shape and form! Let the flames devour them! Let the pike and cap of Liberty, the plough and the ear of corn, and the emblems of every trade by which society is enriched and embellished, henceforth be the only heraldry of the Republic!

Then taking a lighted torch he set fire to the wood pile. At this moment 3,000 birds were released, each having tied around its neck a tricolor ribbon with the words, "We are free—be like us!"

The fourth stop was at the Invalides where there was a colossal statue representing the French people crushing Federalism. An inscription on the base read, "Aristocracy has appeared under a hundred different forms, but the almighty people have everywhere crushed it." Here the President heaped curses upon the monster of Federalism.

Finally the procession reached the Champ de Mars where two figures symbolic of Liberty and Equality stood. Suspended between them was a huge plane, the national plane which was to bring all men to the same level. Here the President announced the result of the votes accepting the Constitution saying, "A year ago our territories were occupied by the foe; we proclaimed the Republic and we were victorious." Then the urn containing the ashes of the dead heroes was the object of an extended ritual which concluded the program at the Champ de Mars. Following were a fraternal banquet, singing, dancing and a military pantomime of the siege of Lille which excited the emotions of the spectators.

Four new Gossec band compositions received their premiere as part of this great festival. The first was sung at the site of the Bastille, the *Hymn of Liberty,* w. 89. This is truly an inspired work of real musical interest. It is in three movements and the text deals entirely with Nature. A government document exists for the copying of parts for this and two more works for this festival, the *Hymn of Nature,* w. 90, and the *Air des Marseillais* for band and chorus, w. 93. It tells us copyists were paid for some 3,750 pages of music. We may assume the project was late in reaching the copyists for they received an additional allowance of 60 livres "for 20 nights, 6 livres for beer." As the representatives drunk from the cup, at the same site, the *Hymn of Nature,* w. 90, was performed. This composition has all the mindless exuberance of a fraternity song, which was probably appropriate.

It was at the second stop, the triumphal arch, that the *Chorus,* w. 91, was sung, judging by the words, " ... do you hear the clarions. Let us go ... " At the *Place de la Revolution* the *Hymn to the Statue of Liberty,* w. 92, was performed, a rather nice, affectionate work. The final music which can be identified with this ceremony was the Gossec arrangement of the famous *Marseillais,* w.93, for band and chorus.

The Development of the Musical Institutions

The National Institute of Music

By November 1793 Sarrette had apparently decided the long range fortunes of his bandsmen lay with an association with the national government, rather than the civic establishment. Thus in a dramatic stroke, Sarrette took the entire band into the Convention Hall itself on November 8, 1793, to appeal for the establishment of a National Institute of Music.

An introductory speech was made by a municipal deputy who said in part, "The artists of the Music of the National Guard whose talents cannot be found elsewhere in Europe come here in order to solicit everything which can contribute to the glory of the Republic."[70] This brief speech was followed by the performance of a march, which contemporary newspapers described as "warlike" and having caused considerable enthusiasm among the representatives.

Then Sarrette was introduced and he made the major speech.

> The Music of the National Parisian Guard, formed by the union of the finest artists in Europe in the field of wind instruments, asks for the establishment of a national music institution where, under the auspices of the Republic, the artists will be able to maintain and improve their knowledge ...
>
> The triumph of Liberty must be noticed in our Festivals ... The soul of the French people which has recovered its first majesty must not be softened by effeminate days spent in the sitting rooms of the palace or in the temples consecrated by the imposture of organized religion. The divinity of the

[70] I am indebted to David Swanzy for a copy of this and subsequent speeches given on this occasion.

Republic is the liberty, its Empire is the whole world. Its services must be held under the celestial vault. The large arenas, the public places hence must be theaters for concerts of a free people.

The musicians have two primary functions—the operation of a music school and performances in the public festivals. Concerning education, the result we obtained in the music academy formed under the auspices of the municipality shows what this kind of institution can become if it is developed by more powerful means.

The artist who are so indispensable for the performance in our national holidays will be trained in that institute. There will be three or four hundred musicians placed in the heart of the Republic, who will be sent to the festivals celebrated throughout the Republic, and they will bring character and energy there.

The union of the artists in the National Guard, dominated by the principles of liberty and equality, performs all of its civic duties. These artists know how to cultivate their art and how to make it deserve a place in the public education with the national confidence; it could not be considered as an academic union, stagnating in ignorance and presumption: they were active, working without jealousy and their only desire was to perfect the knowledge of their art.

Let the National Convention decide and the art of music will be continued by emulation. The French Republic will have its own school and we won't have to borrow this kind of music from the softened and slave Italy. We will nationalize the talents which are so useful for our festivals. Even the dominated Germany will be able to celebrate with festivals when they have broken their infamous chains.

In a newly-created national institute we will not only participate in the festivities of the public holidays, but we will also perform magnificent public concerts. The result of this kind of institution will be invaluable because it will give large numbers of young boys and girls the opportunity to adorn our plays and our celebrations, no less magnificent than the spectacles of Greece where music and poetry were majestic ornaments.

Liberty reigns in a republic which is established on virtue ... The last and more interesting motive of this institution will be found in the ones who, trained in the institute, will have a less transcendent talent. They will join that part of the society which, after having worked hard at their various jobs, will celebrate the virtues and the favors of the revolution under the holy tree of liberty.

Sarrette's speech was hardly needed, for most of the representatives were already convinced of the contribution of the band to the revolutionary scene. Nevertheless, the President followed with further praise and then one of the members, M.-J. Chénier, who had written several of the poems used by Gossec, rose to speak.

> I don't need to speak of the civic duty these musicians have given in several circumstances ... I won't speak about the fortunate effect produced by their music ... Their example proves it more than anything I could say. I change the request of the petitioner into a motion and I ask you to vote it right away.

The motion was immediately adopted, but it would take many months of bureaucratic infighting before the motion could be converted into reality. One question was raised regarding the band's appearance at the "unofficial" ceremony of April 15, 1792, but this was defended by several speakers.

One of the members of the band invited the representatives to attend a forthcoming concert on November 20 as proof of their excellence and of the excellence of their teaching. This was followed by the performance of two Gossec hymns, which cannot now be identified.

After this performance, Sarrette spoke again saying that the students would also like to perform.

> Our former despot did not know enough to employ French talent; he looked for artists in Germany. Under the reign of Liberty, we must find most talent among French people.

The students then performed a symphony for band and concluded the day with "Ça ira."

The Concert of November 20, 1793

The concert mentioned above was held in the Feydeau Theater as scheduled. The reader will recall that it was a stipulation of the establishment of the Free Music School that an annual public concert be given. We are fortunate that the entire program was reproduced in the *Journal de Paris* the following day.[71]

[71] Quoted in Swanzy, "The Wind Ensemble and its Music During the French Revolution," 72–73.

> Never before has Paris presented such a complete gathering of talents of the first order in the field of wind instruments; people have never heard such lovely music with such effectiveness. The works performed were:
>
> *Overture* (w. 25 by) Catel, student of Gossec, with an absolutely new character. Its results are terrific.
>
> *Symphonie concertante* for flute, oboe, horn and bassoon by Devienne, performed by the composer, Sallantn, F. Duvernoy and Ozi with such perfection that we would not have imagined it within the capabilities of these artists had we not known that anything is possible to artists who do not disdain polishing the gifts of nature by constant practice.
>
> *Symphonie concertante* (w. 72) for wind instruments, in which the famous Gossec joined together the merits of a difficult and harmonious composition, full of life and grace.
>
> *Hymne patriotique* (w. 35) by Catel in which we have noticed how pleasing the accompaniment of all the wind instruments is for the listeners; its sound, which is similar to the sound of the voices themselves, makes the harmony parts easier to hear.
>
> *March funèbre* (w. 75) by Gossec.
>
> *O salutaris* by Gossec, transcribed for three horns.
>
> *Trio* for clarinets and bassoon by X. Lefèvre.
>
> *Ronde nationale* (w. 85) by Gossec.
>
> *Hymn of Liberty* (probably w. 89) by Gossec.

We may assume that both faculty and students performed on this concert, because in addition to the artists mentioned by newspapers Sarrette would surely have wanted to demonstrate the effectiveness of the teaching. Sarrette also used the occasion, in view of the representatives being in attendance, to make a long speech during intermission. The text for this speech is lost, but Pierre has constructed a large portion of it from quotations in newspapers.[72]

[72] Pierre, *B. Sarrette*, 48–51.

This music must be considered in three different ways, in the public festivals, as military music and in the field of education. There is no Republic without national holidays and no national holiday without music. The first of these truths is proved by the kind of government and by the example of all the peoples who preceded us. This truth has been felt so deeply that a decree established celebrations in a very positive way.

Everyone knows the effects of music and its power over the spirit. Instruction is very necessary because not all music prompts the result we expect for the festivals and battles, and further, all the instruments must not be used indifferently. The composers discuss their works in the Institute and they adopt or reject the different characters which can be given to their compositions according to the expected result. In the same Institute we train the students for performance in our festivals. Others are trained who must be sent to the departments for their festivals or to the armies to entertain the warlike spirit in the garrison and in battle.

Because the public spectacles must be guided in order to excite and keep the republican spirit in the souls of the spectators, music has an important role, and education will help us to place well-trained musicians in these various public festivals.

Because the national holidays can only be held in the open air, stringed instruments cannot be used. The quality of their sound does not allow them to be heard. We must then prefer the wind instruments only, over which the atmosphere does not have the same influence; their volume of sound is eight times greater than the volume of stringed instruments.

This institute has already proved its usefulness not only through the musicians it has trained, but also by its discoveries in the instrumental area. The composers, who are accustomed to producing music for the theaters and concert halls, noticed that they did not have the same results in open air when the same instruments were used. They searched for a solution. From the ancient Greeks they reconstructed the tuba curva and from the Jews the buccin. The tuba curva was part of the ornaments of the ancient coach of Voltaire. Its given shape and dimensions were calculated by the composers, and the sound which was needed was produced very successfully. The second instrument, the buccin, produces an absolutely new and terrible sound. We can hear this instrument at a quarter of a lieue away. There are only three notes possible, but a construction allows the musician to change pitch. We know that the clarinet took the place of the clarion with a great advantage because the sound of the clarion was too harsh. One of our musicians has invented a counter-clarion for the bass part, but this instrument is yet to be perfected.

A few additional topics discussed by Sarrette are mentioned in the *Paris News*. He mentioned again that now it was no longer necessary to import musicians from Germany and Italy. He indicated that in the beginning students were admitted on a geographical basis, three from each section, but now they were admitted only on the basis of talent. This same paper also observed that Sarrette and his men gave evidence of being happier than most of their contemporaries at this time, an observation the paper apparently took to be evidence of their good work. The paper also expressed its appreciation for Gossec and for the "young Catel who escaped our applause because of his modesty."

On the day following this concert, the Committee of Public Instruction added thirteen artists to the faculty on a provisional basis:

Composers: 125 livres per month
J. François Lesueur
Étienne Méhul

Teachers of the First Class: 71 livres
Frederic Blasius, violin
Pierre Blasius, violin
Jacques Cornu, serpent and bassoon
Henry Domnich, horn
François Gebuer, bassoon
Alexandre Hardy, bassoon
Rudolphe Kreutzer,[73] violin
Henry Lavasseur, cello
Pierre Marciliac, solfeggio and trombone
Joseph Rogat, solfeggio and bassoon
François Sallantin, oboe

In subsequent months piano fauclty and more composers (Cherubini, Duret, Dalayrac, L. Jadin, H. Jadin, Berton and Rode) would be added making appropriate the change of name in 1795 to Conservatory.

[73] The same man immortalized by the composition of Beethoven.

Musique à l'usage des fêtes nationales

ON JANUARY 10, 1794, Sarrette presented to the Committee of Public Instruction a proposal for the foundation of an association of composers in order to control the profit taking of local music stores with regard to the music used at festivals. The Committee agreed and set up a plan whereby the association would provide the government each month with 550 copies of its issue, the publication to be called the *Musique à l'usage des fêtes nationales.* The first issue was printed on April 9, 1794, and would run through twelve volumes with as many as eight compositions per volume. This idea led in turn to the Committee of Public Safety extending the idea in an attempt to use the publication for propaganda purposes. Thus, in the coming months it would frequently subsidize the Association for the publication of thousands of additional copies of hymns for distribution throughout Paris.

The Arrest of Sarrette

THE "TERROR" WAS A PERIOD during which almost no public official was immune from fear; any seen or unseen enemy might affect one's arrest on the suspicion of counter-revolutionary activities. On March 25, 1794, Sarrette himself was arrested and would not be released until May 10, 1794. The "official" charge was that he had incarcerated people in his home, including one lady for three days, in what he called "the discipline prison of the National Guard Music." The real reason might have been that Sarrette did in fact hide J.-H. Chénier in his house while the latter was in disfavor with Robespierre, thus saving his life.

In any case, the authorities locked up Sarrette and then searched his papers looking for suspicious documents by which they could justify the imprisonment. The fact that they could find nothing, the constant pressure on the officials by Sarrette's friends and the approaching Festival of the

Supreme Being, a brain-child of Robespierre, all combined to win his release. One interesting document, by the Institute's secretary, Vény, is still extant and is representative of the efforts of those in the school who urged for Sarrette's release.

> I must remind you that only Sarrette had the direction of this useful institution. Gossec and the other artists, who were his colleagues, spend all of their time in teaching because they trusted in Sarrette for the administration and the continuation of the Institute he had founded.
>
> For a month I have been able to take the place of Sarrette because I know almost everything about his actions. If, in order to continue my own obligations I cease to carry out his functions, this institution will surely meet a lot of troubles. I foresee the necessity of this ... and in order to maintain the Institute, I request that Sarrette obtain his temporary freedom with a guard for the time of the organization of the music corps will last.

Finally, on May 30, 1794, at 5:50 PM, the National Institute presented a student concert in the Feydeau Theater. A note from Sarrette to the Committee of Public Safety indicates that the concert represented students who had been studying for a year, some of whom were about to leave to join the armies. The works performed included the *Patriotic Chorus*, w. 87, by Gossec, the Méhul *Overture*, w. 142, the *Marche Militaire*, w. 128, by Lefèvre, the *Overture*, w. 54, by Devienne and a *Symphonie concertane* for flute, oboe, horn and bassoon by Geveaux.

Band Music During the Terror

August 1793 – August 1794

On August 30, 1793, a deputy said, "Let Terror be the order of the day," and so it was. The Committee of Public Safety, with Robespierre now the most influential member, in September requested and received from the Convention the Law of Suspects. This allowed for the arrest of anyone who gave sign of opposition to the revolution and began the period with which we associate the use of the guillotine. Death sentences were handed out at the rate of about seven per day including many recent leaders of the revolution itself, causing Vergniaud to say, "The Revolution is devouring its own children."

Civil strife, reverses in the military campaigns and the increasing complex in-fighting on the political front resulted in the Convention being officially set aside. A virtual dictatorship came into existence until July 1794 when Robespierre himself was arrested and sent to the guillotine.

The anti-religious character of the revolution came to a climax in the Fall of 1793. The revolutionary forces had moved early with the elimination of perpetual monastic vows in February 1790 and the Civic Constitution of the Clergy voted in July 1790 which made all priests salaried employees of the state. Church property was sold and in the Fall of 1793 bells and sacred vessels were stripped for the war effort. In the provinces this attitude had the effect of creating a great split in the country for many peasants felt more loyal to the international Church than to the revolutionary government in Paris.

In Paris, which was much more indifferent to religion, a determined effort was made in the Fall of 1793 to de-Christianize the country. There were two rather peculiar manifestations. The first was the declaration of a new calendar, dated back to the establishment of the republic in 1792. Replacing the Christian calendar with its feast days named after the saints was the Revolutionary Calendar in which the months were named for nature, for their typical weather: vintage, mist and frost for Autumn; snow, rain and wind for Winter; budding, flowering and meadows for Spring and harvest, warmth and fruit for Summer! The month was divided into three periods of ten days called *décades,* each ending in a day of rest replacing Sunday, called *décadi.* The remaining five days were declared national holidays, *sans-culottides.* Nature would replace God until 1805 Anno Domini.

Music for the Festival of the Worship of Reason

THE SECOND MANIFESTATION of the new attack on the Christian religion in the Fall of 1793 was the decision to rename all churches "Temples of Reason" and to hold a service in honor of Reason on each *décadi.* This actually happened for a while, but the idea is remembered primarily due to the first of these celebrations, held on November 10, in Notre Dame. A description of the setting is given in a contemporary newspaper.

> When you consider that there is no absurdity anywhere in the world that has not been seriously preached by the priests, what is the more surprising is not that we have suddenly given up all our superstitious mythology, but that we delayed so long in rejecting them as they deserved. To celebrate this triumph of reason, that we have so long awaited, the department and Commune of Paris decreed that there should be a patriotic celebration on the following *décadi.*
>
> In the former metropolitan church of Paris, an immense crowd assembled. There they had erected a temple of simple

but majestic architecture, on whose facade could be read the words, "to philosophy." They had decorated the entrance of this temple with busts of the *philosophes* who had contributed by their enlightenment to the advent of the present Revolution. In the sacred temple was raised the summit of a mountain. Toward the center, upon a rock, was seen burning the torch of Truth. All the constituted authorities were represented in this sanctuary. The only one not there was the armed force, and the commandant general, in his order of the day, anticipated those who had noticed this by pointing out that arms belonged only to battles, and not where brethren came to cleanse themselves of all their gothic prejudices, and to savor, in the joy of a soul fulfilled, the sweetness of equality.[74]

[74] *Les Revolutions de Paris* (November 13, 1793), quoted in J. Gilchrist, *The Press in the French Revolution* (London: Cheshire Ginn, 1971), 118–119.

The band performed at the foot of this "mountain." During one of the Hymns two rows of young girls, dressed in white and crowned with oak leaves, descended, torch in hand, from the mountain.

As part of the ceremony the declaration of the rights of man and the constitutional acts were read, news from the armies was analyzed, etc. There was something called a "mouth of Truth," to receive opinions, censures and advice that might be useful to the public. There were also two tribunes, one of aged men and one for pregnant women. The center-piece, however, was the Goddess of Liberty, in this case a role played by an actress from the opera. A contemporary observer describes her role:

Mademoiselle Miillard entered borne on a palanquin, the seat of which was formed of oak branches. Women dressed in white, and wearing tri-colored girdles, preceded her. Popular societies, fraternal societies, revolutionary committees, sections, groups of choristers, singers and opera dancers encircled the throne. With the theatrical cothurni on her feet, a Phrygian cap on her head, her frame scarcely covered with a white tunic, over which a flowing cloak of sky-blue was thrown, the priestess was borne, to the sound of instruments, to the foot of the altar and placed on the spot where the adoration of the faithful so lately sought the mystic bread transformed into a divinity. Behind her was a vast torch, emblematical of the light of philosophy, destined henceforward to be the sole flame of the interior of these temples. The actress lighted this flambeau, Chaumette, a Paris official, receiving the encensoir, in which the perfume of burning, from the hands of two acolytes, knelt and waved it in the air. A mutilated statue of the Virgin was lying at his feet ... Dances and hymns attracted the eyes and ears of the spectators. No profanation was lacking in the old temple.[75]

[75] Alphones de Lamartine, *History of the Girondists* (New York: Harpers, 1854), III, 299–300.

Among the music the band performed for this ceremony must be counted three premieres, the *Ode Patriotique*, w. 35, by Catel, the *Overture*, w. 25, by Catel and the *Overture*, w. 142, by Méhul. The latter two overtures are among the most inspired instrumental works of the entire French Revolutionary repertoire. Also performed was a work for chorus and band and a funeral march by Gossec, neither of which can be specifically identified, and the same composer's harmonization of the *Marseillaise*, w. 93.

Celebration of the Victory of Toulon

AT THE CULMINATION of a series of military disasters, the French were forced to surrender to the English at Toulon on August 28, an event which had the effect of intensifying the Terror. After a difficult Fall, when Toulon was recaptured from the English on December 18, a wave of enthusiasm swept the nation. On December 24 the Convention decreed a celebration in honor of the victory and David was again called upon to plan the event.

The parade began with a salvo of artillery from the west end of the Ile de Paris, at 7:00 AM on the morning of December 30, 1793.

> First in the order of march came a detachment of cavalry, preceded by trumpeters. Then 48 cannon, drawn by artillerymen of the sections, groups of citizens representing Popular Societies, Revolutionary Committees, the law-courts, the Commune, the department and ministers, all carrying appropriate banners. They were followed by the Conquerors of the Bastille. Then came 14 triumphal cars. In front of them marched girls dressed in white, with tricolor sashes, carrying laurel branches. Between them marched the members of

the Convention, surrounded by a tricolor ribbon—symbol of their unity—held by the oldest and the youngest soldiers in the country. Last of all, preceded by the band of the National Guard, came David's masterpiece, the Car of Victory.[76]

[76] J. M. Thompson, *The French Revolution* (Oxford: Basil Blackwell, 1955), 414–415.

We cannot identify the exact works performed on this day, but a band work with chorus was performed at the first stop, the *Temple de l'Humanité*, and a similar work later at the Champ de Mars. The ceremony ended there with "warlike" music by the band.

Anniversary of the Death of Louis XVI

THE YEAR 1794 opened with a popular, if not national, festival celebrating the first anniversary of the beheading of Louis XVI. Laurent, a member of the Convention, was an eyewitness who left an account of this ceremony.

> The joyful bell announced the solemnity of the day at 7:00 AM. On the Place de la Liberty a shattered and tottering edifice was erected on which were placed the effigies of the allied despots who at this moment are uniting their perfidious efforts against French liberty. The effigy of Capet (Louis XVI) was there as well; such as he was after the nation's sword had fallen on his guilty head. The effigies of these monsters were all drooping, seeming to indicate that they were only awaiting the blow which should hurl them into the abyss. That of Capet was lying down, indicating that he had already been smitten ...
>
> The citizens arrived in great numbers, the constituted authorities arrived, preceded by harmonious music. The signal having been given, two pieces of cannon were fired. Later four detachments of cavalry appeared and fell upon it, saber in hand. Promptly the heads and limbs of the tyrants were scattered, amid the acclamations of the people. Almost at the same time the avenging flames appeared and consumed the disgraced and filthy remains of this monstrous group. The joyful bell sounded anew. Dances were formed around the fire, and the citizens only left it to meet again in the Temple of Reason, there to pass the evening in the pleasures of fraternity and equality.[77]

[77] Quoted in A. Aulard, *The French Revolution* (New York: Russell & Russell, 1965), II, 321.

One band composition, the *Hymn for January 21*, w. 105, by H. Jadin was, we believe, premiered on this day. Unfortunately the original version did not survive, only a version for single voice and six winds.

There are two isolated compositions known to have received their first performance during the Spring of 1794, for which we have no surviving information regarding the occasion. *The Steps of the Republic Charge,* w. 14, a combat song dedicated "to the defenders of the country" by Cambini was announced in the local newspapers on April 6, 1794. Another, announced in June, was the *Song for Freed Slaves*, w. 111, by L. Jadin for voice, 2 clarinets and bassoons. Earlier in the year the Convention abolished slavery and several songs of this nature followed, some making pointed reference to America.

Music for the Festival of the Supreme Being

THE GREATEST OF ALL the French revolutionary festivals, the celebration of the Supreme Being, represented the triumph of the dechristianizing aspect of the Enlightenment. The Committee of Public Instruction began to see that their ideal state of justice and virtue required a central moral force for the foundation of these ideas among the masses. Having discarded the Roman Catholic faith, and having mixed success with the substitution of the worship of Reason, a new alternative was clearly needed—a means of supplying both the people's longing for God and immortality and the state's desire to foster patriotism.

Robespierre announced the new philosophy in a major speech on May 7, 1793, dealing with the subject, "The relationship between religion and moral ideas and Republic principles." To create a philosophical basis for the new God, Robespierre reached back to the *Contrat Social* of Rousseau, who had argued not for a national religion, but a State religion.

There is a profession of faith of which it pertains to the sovereign to determine the articles, not precisely, as dogmas of religion, but as sentiments of sociability, without which it is impossible to be a good subject and a faithful citizen.[78]

After praising Rousseau, Robespierre began,

What is there in common between the priests and God? The priests are to morality what quacks are to medicine. How different is the God of Nature to the God of the priests! I know nothing that so nearly resembles atheism as the religions which they have framed. By grossly misrepresenting the Supreme Being, they have annihilated belief in Him as far as lay in their power. They made Him at one time a globe of fire, at another an ox, sometimes a tree, sometimes a man, sometimes a king. The priests have created a God after their own image; they have made Him jealous, capricious, greedy, cruel and implacable; they have treated Him as the mayors of the palace formerly treated the descendants of Clovis, in order to reign in His name and to put themselves in His place, they have confined Him in heaven as in a palace, and have called Him to earth only to demand of Him for their interest tithes, wealth, honors, pleasures and power. The real temple of the Supreme Being is the universe; His worship, virtue, His festivals, the joy of a great nation, assembled in His presence, to knit closer the bonds of universal fraternity, and to pay Him the homage of intelligent and pure hearts.[79]

Robespierre, in the course of the speech, laid out a simple definition: [1] The French people recognized the existence of a Supreme Being and the immortality of the soul, [2] the kind of worship best suited to this Supreme Being consisted in doing one's duties, [3] these duties included hating bad faith, traitors, etc., doing good to one's neighbor and never being unjust, etc., and [4] festivals would be the vehicle to keep these ideas before the common man.

Hence all France began to prepare for local festivals celebrating the Supreme Being, to be held on June 8, 1794. In Paris the entire populace seemed to get into the spirit of the planning. A contemporary newspaper recalls the atmosphere of the day itself.

The public spirit developed in a way that was as satisfying as it was powerful. Without contradiction, this day consecrated

[78] Quoted in Aulard, *The French Revolution*, III, 184.

Figure 12: View of the Tuileries Gardens on the day of the Festival of the Supreme Being, June 8, 1794.

[79] Quoted in Thiers, *History of the French Revolution*, III, 377–378.

to the Supreme Being will be the finest day in the life of the virtuous man, and it will always be with renewed interest, with the most lively sentiment that he will recall this happy occasion.

One saw nothing here of the pomp of courts and the ruinous display of despots. Festoons, garlands of flowers, numerous foliages, trees planted before every door and everywhere the gay national colors fluttering in the breeze: at first sight one would have said that Paris had changed into a vast and beautiful garden, into a smiling orchard.[80]

[80] *Le Journal de la Montagne,* June 10, 1794, quoted in Gilchrist, *The Press in the French Revolution,* 119.

The diary of a private citizen captures this same excitement on a more personal level.

On the 7th all citizens had been invited to adorn their houses with garlands and oak branches for the celebrations in honor of the Supreme Being. The night of the 7th and 8th was an almost sleepless one for me, because of the pleasures awaiting me. On the 8th we were all awake before 5:00 AM; at 6:00, I got up. I wore an overskirt of lawn, a tricolor sash round my waist, and an embroidered fichu of red cotton; on my head, a cambric fichu, arranged like the fillet round the brows of Grecian women, and my hair, dressed in nine small plaits, was upswept on to the crown of my head. In our pockets we stuffed some slices of bread and some cooking-chocolate. At 8:00 we set off for the National Garden, each of us bearing an oak branch in her hand.[81]

[81] Quoted in Jean Robiquet, *Daily Life in the French Revolution* (New York: Macmillan, 1965), 133–134.

The official observance began at the National Gardens, the Tuileries. Here a kind of stadium had been built, with special seating for the Convention. On an almost throne-like seat, higher than those of the Convention, would sit Robespierre. Bas-reliefs had been constructed by David representing justice, virtue, fidelity and the French people vanquishing their enemies. Also visible were a statue of liberty, a small tree covered with tricolored leaves, and a superb chariot with eight oxen with gilden horns on which was displayed a group of agricultural and mechanical objects. The center piece, in front of Robespierre's seat, was a colossal group of figures representing atheism, egotism, nothingness, crimes and vice. The plan was for Robespierre, at the end of the Tuileries portion of the celebration, to light these figures made of combustible materials, and as they were destroyed a statue of Wisdom would come into view.

Robespierre arrived, carefully dressed to set himself apart from the rest of the Convention, carrying an enormous bouquet of flowers and wheat-ears, for the opening speech.

> Frenchmen, republicans! at length has arrived the day forever fortunate, which the French people have consecrated to the Supreme Being! Never did the world which he has created offer to its Author a spectacle more worthy of his regard. He has seen reigning over the earth tyranny, crime, imposture. He sees at this moment an entire nation contending against all the oppressors of the human race, suspending the course of their heroic labors, to raise their thoughts and views toward the Great Being who gave them the wisdom to undertake and the force to execute them!
>
> He did not create Kings to devour the human species; he did not create priests to harness us like vile animals to the chariot of kings, and give to the world the example of baseness, pride, perfidy, avarice, debauchery and falsehood; but he created the universe to make known his power, he created men to aid and love each other, and to attain happiness by the path of virtue.[82]

[82] Quoted in de Lamartine, *History of the Girondists*, 444.

After a lengthy speech in this style, there was a pause for music, the *Hymn to the Supreme Being*, w. 96, by Gossec, a work expressly written to be performed by the attending public. There is a popular belief that the bandsmen and students of the Institute had gone throughout the city in the preceding days to teach this Hymn to the public, although there is no evidence to confirm this. There is evidence to suggest that there were careful rehearsals; one was held three days before, from 7:00 to 10:00 PM, and another two days before at 3:00 PM for school children.

After the music was concluded, Robespierre descended from the stadium to set fire to the group representing atheism. An ill-wind left the emerging statue of Wisdom blackened with smoke, to the delight of those gathered. Robespierre continued with his second speech at this location.

> The monster that the genie of kings vomited out on France has returned to the void. With him may all crimes and all

of the ills of the world disappear. Armed alternatively with the daggers of fanaticism and the poisons of atheism, kings always plot the assassination of humanity. If they can no longer disfigure the divinity by superstition and compound it with their crimes, they labor to banish it from the earth in order to reign alone with their crime.[83]

[83] Quoted in Jean Matrat, *Robespierre* (New York: Scribner's, 1971), 258.

Now the procession was formed for the walk to the Champ de Mars, which began at noon. First the members of the Convention, with their leader several steps in front, followed by the oxen cart. Next came the public, the men on one side of the street, the women on the other side and the children in the middle. According to David's master plan the band led the parade "playing patriotic tunes," and included in the parade were the music students of the Institute "with a hundred drums."

At the Champ de Mars stood the piece de resistance; a huge mountain which had been constructed from the materials and earth which had previously been the Altar of the Fatherland. The size of this mountain can be gained by considering that during the ceremony not only did Robespierre and the entire Convention stand upon it, together with a large corps of professional musicians but also a special chorus of 2,400 citizens, ten old men, ten mothers, ten young girls, ten young men, and ten little boys from each of the forty-eight wards of Paris. A contemporary described the sight.

> You cannot imagine what a sight it was. It seemed as if someone had transported a huge cliff from the Pyrenees to the middle of the Champ de Mars. On its peak was an obelisk surmounted by a statue of Liberty and Equality. The Hymn was played at 6:30 PM. After each stanza the Champ de Mars re-echoed with shouts of "Viva la Republique!" and there were girls everywhere strewing flowers. My hair was simply full of them. After the ceremony, which finished at 7:00, we were just dying of hunger, thirst and fatigue.[84]

[84] Quoted in Robiquet, *Daily Life in the French Revolution*, 135.

The Hymn referred to here was a new one by Gossec, the *Hymn to the Supreme Being*, w. 95. Contrary to many volumes of literature discussing this ceremony, the text sung was not by Chénier. There *was* a text by Chénier, which was in fact published in the newspapers of the time. Robespierre, with whom Chénier was out of favor as a former Girondin, demanded that another work be performed in the ceremony. Gossec was able to find a poet who could write another text to the music already composed, and his name was Desorgues, a hunchback. This Hymn is a very simple one and seems intended for the large choral forces, in which case it would no doubt sound very noble. It appears that a symphony, which cannot be identified was also performed at his point in the ceremony.

One writer makes a fascinating speculation that this mountain was an idea which came from Rosicrucian philosophy. Specifically, he points to a book, *Secret Symbols*, which was republished in 1785, which contains an "alchemist's mountain," as a symbol of regeneration to the Rosicrucians. This Festival of the Supreme Being was also a festival of regeneration, but there were additional resemblances.

> Both mountains have symbolic trees planted at various levels. Both have a smoking tripod or alchemist's kiln. Both have some sort of balustrade encircling the summit. Both show a supreme device: the Rosicrucians have a crown and orb and a Tree of Life; the Revolutionaries a Tree of Liberty.[85]

[85] John Carr, *Robespierre* (London: Constable, 1972), 83–84.

In conclusion, one must note that this ceremony failed to have the great effect of binding the country together which the Committee and Robespierre had hoped for. Robespierre himself made additional enemies by his very prominent role, not to mention those who could find here many philosophical ideas to oppose. On an individual level, however, it must have been a moving occasion for many of those 100,000 who observed it. One middle-class worker from the Guillaume-Tell section wrote,

> I do not think that there has ever been such a day in the whole of human history. It was sublime, both in a physical and in a moral sense. Men with sensitive minds will cherish its memory for the rest of their lives.[86]

[86] Quoted in Albert Soboul, *The French Revolution* (New York: Randam House, 1975), 399.

Music for the Celebration of Victories

UNTIL THIS TIME, the nature of the ceremonies which the band participated in were highly specialized, rather carefully planned events. The choral and band music was almost always composed for the specific ceremony in question. Gradually, of course, a body of literature had accumulated which allowed the musicians to provide music on a more spontaneous basis. Such would be the case in the Summer of 1794.

The French armies achieved two victories in the Summer of 1794 of not only military significance but of great political impact. The first was the Battle of Fleurus, fought on June 26 by the armies under General Jourdan. This victory, during which by the way both balloons and semaphore were used for the first time, opened the Belgium frontier and greatly relieved the political pressure in this area. Indeed, the immediate impact was no further excuse for "The Terror" and Robespierre soon fell from power.

The Convention heard of this victory on June 29 and scheduled a victory celebration for the same evening, to be held in the Tuileries, the national gardens. In addition to the usual marches which the band must have now had available in considerable number there were some vocal compositions performed as well. The Catel *Hymn to Victory*, w. 38, seems to have been written and performed on this same day. This represents no particular surprise for it is for single singer and band and is brief and simple. A portion of another work, probably just the first movement, by Catel, the *Battle of Fleurus*, w. 39, was also performed at this ceremony. This three-movement work, which is one of the very best and most inspired of the repertoire, received its first complete performance on July 14. It must also be pointed out that the *Overture*, w. 26, by Catel seems to have been originally associated with this larger choral work. On one of the manuscript parts for the *Overture* is found a note reading, "Overture which precedes the three choirs of the battle of Fleurus."

However, this very interesting work seems more appropriate to the later ceremony on July 14 and we assume it was first performed there as well. Finally, it is possible that the Cambini *Ode on the Victory won in the fields of Fleurus,* w. 17, also was performed on June 29.

Similarly, the battle which resulted in the fall of Ostende was celebrated on July 4, 1794, in the Tuileries in another hastily organized appearance by the band. In this case a rather impressive concert could be given as a number of compositions were at this moment in rehearsal for the annual celebration of the fall of the Bastille on July 14. No doubt the repertoire was very similar to the celebration of June 29. There seems to have been, however, the first performance of a major new work, the *Le Chant du départ,* w. 143, of Méhul. Here is a work which to this observer seems of little interest, even boring, yet which in its time was of great popularity and might be said to have been the only rival to the *Marseillaise* itself. It is for solo voice and is scored for instrumentation more appropriate for a field band than the Paris one: 2 clarinets, 2 trumpets, 2 bassoons, serpent and timpani.

There is a rather attractive story told about the origin of *Le Chant du départ.* Apparently during the time M.-J. Chénier was hiding from Robespierre by living in a basement room in the house of Sarrette, he was inspired—partly from concern for his brother who was also sought by Robespierre—by news of the victories to write the poem. Méhul, who came to visit him, was given the poem, was in turn inspired and went immediately upstairs, where he wrote the music during the general noise of conversation—standing and using for a writing surface the mantel of a fireplace. Sarrette, when the right moment presented itself, gave the work to Robespierre as the work of a poet who wished to remain unknown. Robespierre is said to have exclaimed, "At this happy hour, voila, grand and Republican poetry has appeared." It was only after Robespierre's fall at the end of July that the true poet could be identified.

Finally, a copyist's note reveals that a set of parts was made of the Gossec *Hymn to Liberty*, w. 88, for performance at this celebration on July 4, 1794.

Music for the Fifth Anniversary of the Bastille

THE ANNUAL CELEBRATION of the fall of the Bastille was held in this year in the Tuileries, which was lighted specially for the evening concert. The Champ de Mars was unusable due to its condition after the Festival of the Supreme Being the previous month. Perhaps to make up for the lack of the traditional setting, the Committee of Public Instruction approved a budget which would allow for the participation of 240 instrumentalists, a large number of whom were hired from various theater orchestras in Paris. This body of musicians included for the first time string players, for the performance of the Chorus from *d'Ernelinde*, the Overture to *d'Iphigenie*, at least one movement from a Haydn *Symphony in C* and a quasi music drama called *The Fall of the Bastille*.

The band performed the now lost *Overture to Démophon*, w. 158, by Vogel, the Gossec *Hymn to Liberty*, w. 88, and *Hymn to the Supreme Being*, w. 95, Catel's *Hymn to Victory*, w. 39, Méhul's *Chant du départ*, w. 143, the *Battle of Fleurus*, w. 39, the *National Round*, w. 85, by Gossec and, of course, the *Marseillaise*. Regarding this concert there is extant one document,[87] a bill by the Opera copyist, Lefevre, for the copying of parts for the Catel, *Battle of Fleurus* (see Table 1).

Two additional works are mentioned in the printed program of this ceremony, which are now lost: the *March of the Sans-Culottides*, w. 4, and the *March of the Armies of the Republic*, w. 3.

The Celebration of August Tenth

THE CELEBRATION of the fall of the monarchy, which had been scheduled to be an annual national celebration, was

Table 1: A bill by the Opera copyist, Lefevre, for the copying of parts for the Catel, *Battle of Fleurus*.

Chorus	
haute-contre	15
alto	15
bass	20
Band	
flute (1st & 2nd)	6
clarinet (1st & 2nd)	8
horn (1st & 2nd)	6
trumpet (1st & 2nd)	4
trombone (3 parts)	3
bassoon (1st & 2nd)	8
serpent	10
string bass	6
timpani	6
bass drum & cymbal	6

[87] Quoted in Pierre, *Les Hymnes*, 333. Pierre also quotes an additional document regarding the rehearsals of this work, in a note sent to a member of the Committee for Public Instruction: *We notify you that tomorrow the 12th several artists will be rehearsing the Bataille de Fleurus, a large chorus which will be performed on the concert on the 14th. If your schedule will permit you to attend this rehearsal, which will take place at the Institute, we invite you to come there at 8:00 AM.*

only hastily organized due to the political chaos surrounding the fall of Robespierre a fortnight before. For the same reason accounts of the festival are very incomplete. We do know that it was again held in the Tuileries and that it consisted primarily of a concert by the band, followed by dancing by the public. The program included the Méhul *Chant du départ*, w. 143, for which we have an extant review.

> But the work which produced general enthusiasm was the *Chant de guerre* by Chénier and Méhul. You undoubtedly recall the eulogy by Plato, in his *Livre des lois,* and Plutarch in his *Opuscules* produced at this Tyrtee verses which burned and the nervous animation of the music contributed to the success of the Spartans against the Messeniens. When one hears the *Chant du départ,* one thinks one hears the Athenian poet with these words: Tremble enemies of France ... the rage was painted in all the faces, and the spectators appeared all agitated.[88]

This same paper also commented on Catel, as composer of the *Battle of Fleurus,* w. 39, which received another performance on August 10.

> This young composer who marches in the footsteps of his master (Gossec) has seized all the nuances of the poem by Lebrun. He has painted with striking truthfulness the combat, the "recit" of the combat and the song of victory, certainly he must have received from Nature an uncommon and extraordinay amount of energy to render this couplet worthy of Pindare: *Pareils aux flots.*[89]

A copyist's note for this work, for this performance, gives the choral forces the same as in the performance of July 14, but the band is somewhat larger (see Table 2).

We have an additional clue to the size of the band used for this ceremony in a copyist's note for a work which received its first performance on this day, Méhul's *Hymn of Victories,* w. 144. It seems obvious from this that the work was begun with one of the earlier victory celebrations in mind. However, textual references to the fall of Robespierre prove that it was not finished in time, whereas the performance on August 10 can be documented by the newspapers (see Table 3).

[88] Duchosal, Quoted in Pierre, *Les Hymnes,* 346.

[89] Ibid., 336.

Table 2: Copyist's note for the Catel *Battle of Fleurus* for performance on August 10.

flute (1st & 2nd)	8
clarinet (1st & 2nd)	14
horn (1st & 2nd)	6
trumpet (1st & 2nd)	4
trombone (3)	4
bassoon (1st & 2nd)	8
serpent	8
string bass	10
tympani	2
bass drum & cymbal	2

Table 3: Copyist's note for the Méhul *Hymn of Victories,* w. 144, performance on August 10.

flute	6
clarinet	14
trumpet	4
horn	6
trombone	3
bassoon	8
serpent	6
string bass	6
buccin, large drum and cymbal	

Works for band and chorus which were heard again in this concert include works by Gossec, *Hymn to the Supreme Being*, w. 95, and *Hymn to Equality*, w. 90 (previously called *Hymn to Nature*), and Catel's *Hymn to Victory*, w. 38. Two large purely instrumental works were performed as well, the Méhul *Overture*, w. 142, and a new work, the Gossec *Symphony in C*, w. 71, which is certainly one of his best instrumental compositions. Perhaps it is in reflection of these last two works that the newspaper, *Duchosal*, wrote the following after this concert:

> The instruments performed with a perfection previously unknown, and certainly even Böece (Boethius) himself, if he had heard the artists of the National Institute would not have been able to prevent himself from looking at them as musicians—although he would not wish to attach this name to those who only practice music by the "Ministry of Fingers and Voice."

Band Music After the Terror

September 1794 – December 1795

AFTER THE FALL OF ROBESPIERRE there was a widespread feeling among politicians that the time was approaching when the Revolution should be brought to some kind of conclusion and the period of violence ended. This did not prove easy to do, however, for the long period of terror had left many divisions. Those who still favored a constitutional monarch suffered a double setback in 1795 with the death of the young son of Louis XVI and the failure of an émigré invasion. This party simply had no candidate to advance.

The result was the reorganization of the government in late 1795 into what would become known as the Directory. A new constitution provided for an executive of five Directors, chosen on the same basis, but differed in age requirements. One-third of the deputies and two of the Directors were to be changed each year.

Music for the Festival of the Fifth Sans-Culottide

This festival was held primarily because it was one of those "extra days" in the new calendar on which national festivals were *supposed* to be held. The previous November the Convention had decided that on this day, for lack of anything to celebrate, a ceremony would be held through which the remains of Marat would be moved to the Panthéon and those of Mirabeau would be removed. By the time (September 21, 1794) the day for the festival came, political opinion was no longer quite in unison with the plans—Marat was no longer quite so holy nor Mirabeau quite the villain. But, rather than cause more political problems than there were, the ceremony went on as scheduled. Because of the recent victories of the armies the celebration of this was thrown into the day's events as well. The result was a ceremony in the Tuileries in honor of the victories, then the march to the Panthéon where additional music would be performed. Because the records are not specific we cannot, today, tell in every case which composition was performed where but we do have a rather complete list of the total repertoire.

One new composition performed on this day was the *Hymn to the Panthéon*, w. 45, by Cherubini. This work and the *Hymn of Liberty*, w. 88, by Gossec which was repeated on this day, we know were part of the ceremonies for Marat at the Panthéon. For these works we also have the copyist's information which indicates the size band used for the ceremony (see Tables 4 and 5).

One cannot say how these lists correspond. Were the Gossec extra parts needed this day, were more Cherubini parts copied than needed? The best guess is that the band was more of the size implied by the Cherubini, as the Gossec seems too small for this date.

There are also surviving documents regarding two earlier compositions which received performances this day, the Méhul *Chant du départ*, w. 143, and the *Hymn of Victories*, w. 144. In the case of these works, the Convention had printed 18,000 copies of the music in honor of the day, 1,000 for the fourteen major armies and the rest for the Convention and the citizens of Paris.

One new composition which was also distributed in mass copies was the *Hymn of Fraternity*, w. 46, by Cherubini. This work seems to have been sung only at the Tuilleries, as part of the victory celebration. A copyist's note tells us the parts copied for September 21, but not the number of each: flute, clarinet, horn, trumpet, bassoon, serpent, contrabass, cymbal, "tambour turc." An additional new composition was the one movement *Symphonie*, w. 107, by Louis Jadin.

Table 4: Copyist information indicating the size of the band used for the ceremony on September 21, 1794.

Gossec

1st clarinet	6
2nd clarinet	7
1st flute	2
2nd flute	2
1st horn	2
2nd horn	2
1st bassoon	2
2nd bassoon	2
serpent	2
trumpet	2
timpani	1

Table 5: Copyist information indicating the size of the band used for the ceremony on September 21, 1794.

Cherubini

1st clarinet	8
2nd clarinet	8
1st flute	3
2nd flute	3
1st horn	4
2nd horn	4
1st bassoon	4
2nd bassoon	4
serpent	4
1st trumpet	2
2nd trumpet	2
trombone	3
contrabasse	12
tuba curva	1
buccin	1
timpani	1
bass drum	2
cymbals	2

Music in Honor of J. J. Rousseau

THE CONVENTION scheduled the 11th of October, 1794, for the moving of the remains of Rousseau to the Panthéon. Virtually nothing is known to the present writer of the actual ceremony, although the text of one of the new compositions written for the occasion may provide a clue. The Gossec *Hymn to J. J. Rousseau,* w. 97, begins with "the old people and mothers" and continues with "representatives of the people," "young girls," etc., alternatively presenting their honors. Gossec, whose inspiration was at best very irregular, was in this case uninspired. This may be the result of the known fact that during the three days he composed the work he was suffering from an inflammation of a tooth.[90]

Another new work, L. Jadin's *Hymn to J. J. Rousseau,* w. 112, is not more successful and has as its claim to fame a trio based on three notes quoted from a composition by Rousseau.[91] The concert also included Lefevre's *March militaire,* w. 128, and an arrangement of Rousseau's *du Devin du Village.*

The final appearance of music at a political event in 1794 was again in honor of victories, this time the armies of Jourdan and Pichegru over the Duke of York. On a motion by Chénier, this type of event was now restricted to a military parade without the elaborate decorations or participation by the Convention. Two new compositions for the occasion, the *Hymn of the Triumphs of the French Republic,* w. 133, by Lesueur and the *Hymn of Victory,* w. 10, by Adrein l'Ainé were performed.

[90] Pierre, *Les Hymnes,* 366.

[91] This famous philosopher began his professional life as a music copyist and composer. Several small scale marches for band are extant.

Music for the Concert of November 7, 1794

TO MEET THE PROVISIONS of the founding of the original music school, Sarrette again organized the annual concert in the Feydeau Theater. After the re-organization of the Conservatory of Music the following year these particular concerts would not be continued.

For three of the band works performed on this concert we have copyist's invoices which list the instrumentation presumably used. These compositions are the Lesueur *Scene Patriotique*, w. 134, the Catel *Patriotic Ode*, w. 35, and *Overture*, w. 26 (see Table 6).

	Lesueur	Catel, *Ode*	Catel, *Overture*
clarinet	20	6	14
flute	4	2	8
oboe	4	-	-
bassoon*	6	6	8
horn	12	4	6
trumpet	4	2	2
serpent	3	3	4
trombone	3	3	3
tuba curva	1	-	-
timpani	1	1	2
contrabass	4	-	4

Table 6: Copyist's note listing the instrumentation of the concert on November 7, 1794.

*Ten more played only with the chorus

The Catel *Overture* and the Lesueur work were newly composed for the concert. The latter work was a massive, almost scene-like episodic work in one movement. Several already known instrumental works were heard again, including the Méhul *Overture*, w. 142, and marches by Gossec, w. 75, and Lefevre, w. 128. The concert also included works with strings.

One newspaper review has survived, that of the *Affiches, annonces*, Nr. 69, November 19, 1794, which, after grumbling about confusion in seating resulting from unreserved seats, noted,

> The exercise of the National Institute of Music which took place the day before yesterday at the Feydeau Street Theater was very enjoyable. A gathering of distinguished artists, a rare perfection of execution and ensemble all made to please the public. We do not address particular praise to each of the artists who composed; all are equally praised, all merit equally the just enthusiasm of the audience.

Six days later the same paper wrote again adding that the Méhul and Catel *Overtures*, "excited the just enthusiasm of the audience."

Anniversary of the Death of Louis XVI

THE YEAR 1795 opened with a very modest celebration of the beheading of Louis XVI. Two new compositions appear in honor of this day, the *Hymn*, w. 130, by Lefevre and the *Verses on the Anniversary of the Just Punishment of the Last King of France,* w. 60, by Feray. A copyist memorandum tells us the instrumentation used for each performance on this day, January 21, 1795.

	Lefevre	Feray
singers	35	38
clarinet	8	12
flute	4	-
oboe	4	4
bassoon	8	6
trumpet	2	-
horn	8	6
trombone	3	-
serpent	4	-
timpani	1	-

Table 7: Copyist's note indicating the instrumentation used for the concert on January 21, 1795.

Music for the Funeral Ceremony in Honor of Feraud

ON MAY 20, 1795, the Convention was invaded by a mob, consisting mostly of women shouting, "Bread and the Constitution of 1793!" in response to a serious economic condition during most of the first half of 1795. One of the members of the Convention was killed and his head was carried around on a pike. The President, Boissy d'Anglas, earned a footnote in history by impassively saluting it.

The Convention planned a ceremony in honor of Feraud for June 2 to be held during the sessions of the Convention. There is extant the actual order to Gossec to compose a work for the occasion, demonstrating how the composers were at the service of the politicians.

> Paris, May 30, 1795
>
> I am ordered, Citizen, by the Committee of Public Instruction to send to you the attached poem on the death of our esteemed and unfortunate colleague, Feraud, who was assassinated at his post.
>
> It is the intention of the Committee that you occupy yourself wholeheartedly to setting this verse to music and having it printed in the number of 2,000 copies, in such a manner that they can be distributed to the membership of the Convention and the public on June 2 in the morning of the day of the funeral ceremony for Representative Feraud. The copies are to be deposited with the Committee.
>
> Greetings, etc.
>
> Massieu

Thus, Gossec had three days to write and have printed his *Funeral Hymn,* w. 98, and the same was the case with Méhul, who contributed another *Funeral Hymn,* w. 145. Additional documents authorize the payment of fifty singers to perform and the payment of five copyists for working through the night.

Music for the Festival of Liberty

ON JULY 27 a small observance of the fall of Robespierre, and the ending of the Terror, was held. Three new compositions were written for this occasion, none of particular interest: *Hymn for July 27,* w. 135, by Lesueur, *Hymn for July 27,* w. 146, by Méhul and the *Humanistic Hymn,* w. 99, by Gossec.

Music for the Celebration of August Tenth

THE ANNUAL CELEBRATION of the fall of the monarchy brought forth three new compositions for band and chorus: the *Hymn for August 10,* w. 42, by Catel, the *Hymn to Liberty,* w. 154, by Henri Rigel, père., and the *Republican Hymn for August 10,* w. 47, by Cherubini. The text by Lebrun of this last work was highly praised by the newspaper, *Decade philosophique,* and it reproached the composer, Cherubini, for not using all the text and for not doing justice to that which he did use. The paper was right, the music is rather weak.

Music in Honor of the Girondins

THE THOUGHTLESS EXECUTION of the Girondins in the Fall of 1793, many of them young men in their twenties, young men of great promise, was now seen in its full perspective and a ceremony was planned to commemorate their death. The compositions performed included the *Hymn of the Twenty-Two,* w. 147, by Méhul, *Shades of the Gironde,* w. 100, by Gossec, and perhaps the *Ode,* w. 41, by Catel. In Strasbourg, where a local festival was given, one heard the *Roland à Roncevaux* by Rouget de Lisle.

Establishment of the Conservatory

AFTER THE TERROR ended with the fall of Robespierre, there was not only a desire to bring to a close all forms of violence among the public, which was still being done in the name of the Revolution, but also a desire to solidify the institutions which had been created by the Revolution. The close relationship which the leading composers and artists had established with the politicians made possible at this time the re-organization of the Institute into a more disciplined and permanent institution under the name known today, the

Conservatory of Music. The organization of the new conservatory is clearly outlined in the Convention's decree, which was dated August 3, 1795.

> Decree Establishing a Conservatory of Music
>
> 1. The Conservatory of Music is established in the commune of Paris for the performance and teaching of music. It shall be composed of 115 artists.
> 2. With regard to performance, it shall be used in celebrating national festivals, with regard to teaching, it shall be responsible for the training of pupils in all branches of musical art.
> 3. Six hundred pupils of both sexes shall receive free instruction in the Conservatory. They shall be chosen proportionately in all the departments.
> 4. Surveillance of all branches of instruction in said Conservatory, and of performances in the national festivals, shall be entrusted to five inspectors of instruction chosen from among the composers.
> 5. The five inspectors of instruction shall be appointed by the National Institute of Arts and Sciences.
> 6. Four professors, chosen without discrimination from among the artists of the Conservatory, shall constitute the administration thereof, conjointly with the five inspectors of instruction. Said four professors shall be appointed and renewed annually by the artists of the Conservatory.
> 7. The administration shall be responsible for the internal regulation of the Conservatory, and for supervising the execution of decrees of the Legislative body or orders of the constituted authorities relative to said establishment.
> 8. Artists necessary to complete the Conservatory may be appointed by competitive examination only.
> 9. The examination shall be judged by the National Institute of Arts and Sciences.
> 10. A national library of music is constituted in the Conservatory; it shall be composed of a complete collection of scores and works dealing with that art, of antique or foreign instruments, and of those useful ones which, because of their perfection, may serve as models.
> 11. Said library shall be public, and shall be open at times determined by the National Institute of Arts and Sciences, which appoints the librarian.

12. The stipend of each inspector of instruction is established at 5,000 livres per annum; that of the secretary at 4,000 livres; that of the librarian at 3,000 livres. Three classes of stipends are established for the other artists: 28 positions at 2,500 livres shall constitute the first class, 54 positions at 2,000 livres the second, and 28 positions at 1,600 livres the third class.

13. The expenses of administration and maintenance of the Conservatory shall be regulated and ordered by the executive power, according to statements furnished by the administration of the Conservatory, such expenses shall be defrayed by the public treasury.

14. After twenty years of service, members of the Central Conservatory of Music shall have one-half their stipend as a pension, after which time, each year of service shall augment said pension by one-twentieth of the said stipend.

15. The Conservatory shall furnish daily a body of musicians for the service of the National Guard in the neighborhood of the Legislative Body.

Personnel

Instruction Professors:

Sol-fa, 14
clarinet, 19
flute, 6
oboe, 4
bassoon, 12
first horn, 6
second horn, 6
trumpet, 2
trombone, 1
serpent, 4
bass trombone, 1
tuba curva, 1
timpani, 1
violin, 8
bass, 4
contrabass, 1
harpsichord, 6
organ, 1
vocalization, 3
chant simple, 4

chant déclamé, 2
accompaniment, 3
composition, 7

Performance Professors:

Director-composers, 5
concertmaster
clarinet, 30
flute, 10
first horn, 6
second horn, 6
bassoon, 18
serpent, 8
trombone, 3
trumpet, 4
tuba curva, 2
bass trombone, 2
triangle, 2
bass drum, 2
nonperformers employed in directing pupils in singing or performing at public festivals, 10

Band Music at the End of the Revolution

December 1795 – 1800

BETWEEN 1795 AND 1797 the Directory struggled to deal with a continuing war, continuing bad harvest and economic problems seemingly beyond the ability of the government to control. The constant problems seemed always to produce a legislative body with deep divisions, not the least of which was a new Jacobinism and a new royalist movement supported by the Catholic Clergy.

Three members of the Directory decided in 1797 to take matters into their own hands. In a show of force they instituted a partial Terror and priests and *émigrés* were again forced out of the country. The aftermath of this action, together with continued economic chaos, made the country less stable than ever. Sieyés, one of the few politicians to survive the entire period, decided yet another *coup d'etat* was needed in the Fall of 1799. To do it he needed the help of a General, whom unfortunately almost had to be Napoleon Bonaparte. From this period we date Napoleon's rule and the Revolution's end.

Music for the décade Festivals

IN THE DECREE OF MAY 7, 1794, establishing the Festival of the Supreme Being, Robespierre at the same time set forth a complex plan of smaller festivals to be held on the day of rest, the tenth day called décade. The variety of subjects is extraordinary.

> To the Supreme Being and to Nature; to the human race; to the French people; to the benefactors of humanity; to the martyrs of liberty; to liberty and equality; to the Republic; to the liberty of the world; to love of country; to the hatred of tyrants and traitors; to Truth; to justice; to modesty; to glory and immortality; to friendship; to Frugality; to courage; to good faith; to heroism; to disinterestedness; to stoicism; to love; to conjugal love; to paternal love; to maternal tenderness; to filial piety; to infancy; to youth; to manhood; to old age; to misfortune; to agriculture; to industry; to our forefathers; to posterity and to happiness.

As it turned out most of these were never held and those which were held were held on a very irregular basis. Although a few were ingeniously organized, they attracted in general only a few curious spectators. The day of the great Revolutionary festival was over.

One category of festival was the Recognition of Victories, to be held annually on May 29. Such a festival was held on this date in 1796 and produced four new band works. Two of them are the final contributions in the choral and band medium by Gossec: the *Hymn of Victory*, w. 101, and the *Hymn for the Celebration of Victory*, w. 102. Also performed for the first time were the *Hymn for the Republican Banquet*, w. 43, by Catel and the *Hymn of Victory*, w. 48, by Cherubini. The only other observance of this festival was on the same date in 1799, when we find two new compositions, the final contributions of Cherubini, the *Festival of Recognition*, w. 53, and the *Ode*, w. 59, by André-Frédéric Eler.

Some of the most peculiar band works of the French Revolution are those written for festivals celebrating Agriculture, first held on June 28, 1796. One of the new compositions for this first festival was Henri Berton's *Hymn for the Festival of Agriculture*, w. 12. This work seems clearly intended as "tongue in cheek" and on the basis of it one would conclude that the whole festival was not meant to be taken seriously. Perhaps it was partially in objection to this character of the music that the poet, Lebrun, wrote the following manuscript note on a published copy of the composition.

> I wrote this ode to celebrate a harvest day, it is not a hymn and the subject is not "susceptible." My work has been entirely mutilated by the music and for the music. It must be printed as I wrote it![92]

On the other hand the *Hymn to Agriculture*, w. 106, by Hyacinthe Jadin and especially the *Hymn to Agriculture*, w. 131, by Xavier Lefevre seem totally serious in intent. An additional work appears for the only other known celebration of this festival, on June 28, 1798, the *Hymn to Agriculture*, w. 138, by Jean François Lesueur.

Two extraordinary festivals were held in 1799, those of Newly Weds, and of Old Age. Of the works written for these festivals only Méhul's *Hymn for the Festival of Marriage*, w. 149, is an effective work. There is a very interesting surviving letter written by the poet of this Hymn, Ducis, to government officials in charge of commissioning these works. It demonstrates the capacity of this music to carry political ideas, here the concept of civil supremacy. It is also interesting here to see the poet trying to bring pressure on the composer he desires to set the hymn to music.

> Paris, October 29, 1798
> Citizen Minister,
> I have just returned from the country, visiting in the home of Director Reveillière Épeaux and I send you the hymn on marriage for the celebration of marriage in small communities. I tried to keep it simple, but not remove a sense of nobleness. Citizen Revellière and his family to whom I read it in an evening were very content with it. He also gave his commendation to my hymn for large towns. But he pointed out to me, alone, that the military state can have a fatal influence on the Republic, as it makes one forget civil authority. It is good to remind the people that their sovereignty is in civil authority and that a man of war is only an executor of the will of the people. This observation seemed very wise to me and therefore I made the necessary additions to my two hymns. I wrote on the 29th of last month to Citizen Méhul asking him instantly if he would sustain my hymns with the power of his music, adding that I wished he would be willing to reply

[92] Facsimile reproduced in Pierre, *Les Hymnes*, 95.

promptly in two words. I have not yet received a reply and that worries me. Would you be willing, Citizen Minister, to indicate your desire to him to see that he takes charge of these two hymns? I feel certain he would not be able to resist the pleasure of doing something agreeable to you. For me, I will always have my sweetest reward in having served my country in having served the demands of a Minister so patriotic, and deserving the vote of an enlightened Judge. Assurances of my profound respect and attachment.
    Ducis[93]

[93] Quoted in Pierre, *Les Hymnes*, 433.

The other surviving band work for this festival, the *Hymne à l'hymen*, w. 152, by Piccinni and the composition for the Festival of Old Age, *Hymn for the celebration of Old Age*, w. 139, by Lesuer, are works of little musical interest.

Music for National Festivals

THE ONLY DATES on which celebrations seemed to fall regularly after the fall of Robespierre were those of July 14 and September 22, the Bastille and the Foundation of the Republic. But even these lost the spontaneous excitement of the earlier versions as they became more and more manifestations of political manoeuvres. In the case of the July 14 celebration of 1797, for example, one group wanted the ceremony again at the Champ de Mars to rekindle public patriotism, while another group, led by Camot, dreaded precisely that effect. This ceremony saw the first use of students of the Conservatory in a public festival. One newspaper, *La Décade philosophique*, wrote the following after hearing Méhul's *La Chant du départ*, w. 143, performed on this day.

> The verses of the women in *La Chant du départ* had never appeared so touching. I was near Méhul when they sang the happy production of his genius. I put my arm around him and pressed him gently. We looked at each other, our eyes humid, for his genius is in his soul and when a soul speaks to him he hears it.[94]

[94] Quoted in Pierre, *Les Hymnes*, 347.

Two new compositions for the celebration of the founding of the Republic appear in 1798; both are by Martini and both are of little musical interest, the *Hymn of the Republic,* w. 140, and the *Triumphal Hymn,* w. 141.

Music for the Ceremony of Campo-Formio

THE NECESSARY MACHINERY was intact of course to organize a special ceremony whenever circumstances dictated. One such ceremony was held at the Palace of the Directory on December 10, 1797, as part of the Signing of the Treaty of Campo-Formio. The greater purpose for this ceremony was to welcome Napoleon back to Paris. Having recently added half of Italy to France, and not yet having begun his disastrous Egypt adventure, he was at the very peak of his influence thus far. An eyewitness describes the scene:

> The Directory gave General Bonaparte a solemn reception which in some respects marked an epoch in the history of the Revolution. They chose for this ceremony the court of the Luxembourg Palace; no hall would have been vast enough to contain the crowd that was attracted; there were spectators in every window and on the roof. The five Directors, in Roman costume, were placed on a stage in the courtyard; near them were the deputies of the Council of the Ancients, the Council of Five Hundred and the Institute.
>
> Bonaparte arrived very simply dressed, followed by his aides-de-camp, all of them taller than he, bent with the respect they showed him. The elite of France, gathered there, covered the victorious general with applause. He was the hope of every man, republican or royalist; all saw the present and the future in his strong hands.
>
> M. de Talleyrand, in presenting him to the Directory, called him the Liberator of Italy and assured them that he detested luxury and splendor, the ambition of vulgar souls, and that he loved the poems of Ossian particularly because they detach us from the earth.[95]

Napoleon responded in part,

> Religion, feudalism, royalty have successively, for twenty centuries past, governed Europe; but from the peace which you have just concluded dates the era of representative governments.

[95] Madame de Staël, *Memoirs,* quoted in Jean Bourgignon, *Napoleon Bonaparte* (Paris: Editions Nationales, 1936), I, 138.

You have succeeded in organizing the great nation, whose vast Territory is circumscribed only because Nature herself has fixed its limits.

You have done more. The two finest countries in Europe, formerly so renowned for the arts, the sciences, and the great men whose cradle they were, see, with the greatest hopes, genius and freedom issuing from the tomb of their ancestors.

These are two pedestals on which the destinies are about to place two powerful nations.[96]

[96] Quoted in Thiers, *History of the French Revolution*, V, 196.

Then, Barras, President of the Directory, spoke commenting on how nice it would be if General Hoche (Napoleon's only real competition) could be here to see his friend and urging Napoleon to go and conquer England next. A new band and chorus work by Méhul was now performed, the *Le chant du retour*, w. 148. This is a rousing fairly lengthy work which must have made a great impression on those assembled. The ceremony closed with two distinguished generals, Joubert, hero of the Tyrol, and Andreossy of the artillery, leading a presentation of battle flags, etc.

Music for Military Funerals

BOTH OF THESE GENERALS, Joubert and Hoche, were killed in battle and given state funerals at which the Guard band would perform. Joubert went riding off into the Battle of Novi saying, "I shall either be killed or be victorious."

The death of twenty-nine year old General Hoche was a particular loss to the nation. As head of the combined armies of the Meuse and the Rhine, he was head of the most extensive force under arms and was the only person who could have given the Directory the necessary support to oppose Napoleon. Because of the suddenness of his death, and his youth, there was a rumor that he was poisoned. This possibility was given further support by the post-mortem which found his stomach full of black spots. Some said the Directory itself was responsible. To this charge Barras, spokesman for the Directory, wrote,

His almost sudden death may doubtless be regarded as supernatural; it has remained unexplained by the physicians. Let us leave to Nature her mysteries, they are real and profound, and can dispense us from always seeking for explanations in men's wickedness.[97]

It was natural for many to assume that Napoleon was somehow responsible for he had the most to gain. He answered,

As there existed a party who seemed to think that all crimes belonged to me, endeavors were made to circulate a report that I had poisoned him. There was a time when no mischief could happen that was not imputed to me. Thus, when in Paris I caused Kleber to be assassinated in Egypt; I blew out Desaix's brains at Marengo; I strangled and cut the throats of persons who were confined in prisons; I seized the Pope by the hair of his head, and a hundred similar absurdities.[98]

In any event, the Directory ordered a magnificent funeral in the Champ de Mars which was attended by an immense crowd. This occasion produced one of the very best band works of the entire French Revolutionary repertoire, the *Funeral Hymn on the Death of General Hoche,* w. 49, by Cherubini. The work begins with an independent funeral march, eloquent and mysterious, which was performed in the actual procession. The first movement, "the young girls," was performed after a speech by Barras, by forty young female students of the Conservatory of Music, dressed in white, bands in their hair, wearing sashes of crepe, coming forward with "timid steps" arranged themselves around the mausoleum.

Following a eulogy by Daunou, the second movement was sung, "the old people," and then the third, "the warriors." A final Allegro is spirited and strong in character and was recalled in an official account as follows:

These last words and the charm with which they are combined with the warlike music which animates them, transformed all the performers, drawing universal applause, and changed suddenly the nature of the general emotion. Magistrates, Citizens, military personnel, all appeared occupied only with honor, with new triumphs, and the memory of the

[97] *Memoirs of Barras* (New York: Harper's, 1896), III, 45–46.

[98] Napoleon in *Las Cases,* quoted in Thiers, *History of the French Revolution,* V, 167.

general who led so many times the republican columns to victory.[99]

[99] Quoted in Pierre, *Les Hymnes*, 403.

Music for the Festival of Liberty and the Arts

FOR ALL THE BATTLES AND WARS Italy had suffered through the ages, for all the armies of many nations who had exacted their spoils of victory, never had she been before conquered by a first-class art lover, as was Bonaparte. Beginning in 1796, all of Italy bore the theft of art masterpieces which were sent to Paris, not the least of which was the famous *Mona Lisa*! No more would French art students have to go to Italy to study, Italy was being brought to Paris.

On July 27, 1798, in an ironic coincidence with the anniversary of the fall of Robespierre, a festival was held by which the public could gaze upon the stolen art.

> Float after float laden with rare and valuable books, manuscripts, medallions, paintings and statuary, plundered by the French republican legions from the libraries, museums, public buildings and squares of the nations of Europe—the laocoön, the Apollo of the Belvedere, the Venus of the Capitol, Titians, Raphaels, Veroneses. Float after float! Ten wagon loads of manuscripts and books, thirty wagon loads of paintings and statuary—the most civilizing possessions nations have—stolen by the armies that were to bring liberty and enlightenment, and paraded before the Paris populace ... accompanied by an honor guard of the professors of the College of France and the Polytechnic Institute, and the conservators of the Paris libraries and museums.

One new band composition was written for the festival, the *Chant dithyrambique*, w. 137, by Lesueur.

As for the Italians, as they watched their treasures leave, they made one of history's great puns using the name of the thief:

> Not all Frenchmen are robbers, but a good part are!
> Non tutti Francesi sono ladroni, ma buona parte!

Part II

A Catalog of the Band Music of the French Revolution

THE PURPOSE OF THIS CATALOG is to provide supplementary information about the individual band compositions which have been mentioned in the historical review of the French Revolution in Part I. Since I have studied all this music, and performed much of it, I have added a category called "Commentary," for the purpose of allowing me the opportunity to pass on my own personal reflections on the individual compositions. Following are the abbreviations used in this catalog.

W

The letter "W" followed by sequential numbers is for the purpose of giving the reader a convenient cross-reference tool.

F-Pn

This is a sigla of the international RISM identification of libraries and stands for the Music Division of the National Library of France in Paris.

D-TROb

The Library of the Bundesakademie für musikalische Jugendbildung in Trossingen, Germany. This library has created a separate collection called the "Whitwell Archiv." The numbers which follow D-TROb in this catalog are their shelfmarks for this collection and are found in their publication, *Archiv David Whitwell, Verzeichnis der Noten* (Music catalog).

US-DW

The occasional use of this sigla is to identify copies of music which I donated to the Bundesakademie Library and are not listed in their published catalog of my collection there. They nevertheless have these compositions and can find them by reference to these numbers used in my own library.

Pierre

The appearance of "Pierre" together with a shelf-mark in F-Pn means that this work is identified only in the books of Constant Pierre. These are shelf-marks now more than 200 years old and I have personally had mixed results by the present staff in Paris in finding this music in their library which has been moved, reorganized and re-cataloged over these many years.

Magasin de musique

The *Magasin de musique* publications were the result of a proposal which came from the composers themselves and made to the Committee of Public Instruction on January 10, 1794, for the purpose of the control of profit taking by local music stores. The government saw this idea as an opportunity for public indoctrination through mass distribution of the music to the public. The first issue, *Musique à l'usage des fêtes nationales*, was published on April 9, 1794, and ran through 12 volumes. But for these publications, a large amount of the band music of the French Revolution would have been lost.

Collection Époques

This collection was organized by François de Neufchateau and intended to be ready for distribution on June 13, 1799. The idea was to make available music which did not appear in the *Magasin de musique*, such as more recent compositions and those suitable for use in small towns. It is my understanding that this collection was never actually published and exists only in the form of a proof sheet in F-Pn.

Dudley

Orchestration in the "Musique d'Harmonie" of the French Revolution, unpublished dissertation (University of Calfornia, 1968), which includes some scores assembled by the author.

Swanzy

The Wind Ensemble and its Music During the French Revolution, 1789-1795, an unpublished dissertation (Michigan State University, 1966), which includes some scores assembled by the author.

W. 1, Anonymous, *Marche religieuse*

Original instrumentation
4 clarinets, 2 horns and 2 bassoons

Source
Mss parts only, F-Pn, Bibl. Cons., *Musique d'harmonie,* paquet 30a (Pierre)

W. 2, Anonymous, *Marche religieuse*

Original instrumentation
4 clarinets, 2 horns and 2 bassoons

Source
Mss parts, F-Pn, Bibl. Cons., *Musique d'harmonie,* paquet 30a (Pierre)

W. 3, Anonymous, *La Pas de charge des Armées de la République*

Original instrumentation
Unknown

Source
Believed to be lost.

Commentary
This music is mentioned in the program for a concert given July 14, 1794 in Paris.

W. 4, Anonymous, *La Pas de charge des Sans-Culottides*

Original instrumentation
Unknown

Source
Believed to be lost.

Commentary
This music is mentioned in the program for a concert given July 14, 1794, in Paris.

W. 5, Anonymous, *Première suite de trois marches et trois pas de manoeuvre*

Original instrumentation

Unknown

Source

Believed to be lost.

Commentary

Mentioned in the *Journal de Paris,* August 29, 1794, in an announcement of the program for a public festival to be held September 3, 1794.

W. 6, Anonymous, *Marche*

Original instrumentation

Piccolo, clarinet in F, 2 clarinets in C, 2 oboes, 2 horns in F, trumpet in Bb, trombone, 2 bassoons, serpent, cymbales, grosse caisse, timpani

Source

Mss parts, F-Pn, Bibl. Cons., *Musique d'harmonie,* paquet 50 (Pierre)

W. 7, Anonymous, *Marche*

Original instrumentation

Piccolo, clarinet in F, 2 clarinets in C, 2 oboes, 2 horns in F, trumpet in Bb, trombone, 2 bassoons, serpent, cymbales, grosse caisse, timpani

Source

Mss parts, F-Pn, Bibl. Cons., *Musique d'harmonie,* paquet 50 (Pierre)

W. 8, Anonymous, *Marche*

Original instrumentation

Piccolo, clarinet in F, 2 clarinets in C, 2 oboes, 2 horns in F, trumpet in Bb, trombone, 2 bassoons, serpent, cymbales, grosse caisse, timpani

Source

Mss parts, F-Pn, Bibl. Cons., *Musique d'harmonie,* paquet 50 (Pierre)

W. 9, Anonymous, *Marche*

Original instrumentation

Piccolo, clarinet in F, 2 clarinets in C, 2 oboes, 2 horns in F, trumpet in Bb, trombone, 2 bassoons, serpent, cymbales, grosse caisse, timpani

Source

Mss parts, F-Pn, Bibl. Cons., *Musique d'harmonie,* paquet 50 (Pierre)

Ferdinand Adrien (1760–1830)

FERDINAND ADRIEN was born in 1760 in Liege, Belgium, the eldest of three brothers who were all singers. He served for six years as a singer and singing teacher at the Conservatorio San Onofrio in Naples, followed by service in France in the court of Count d'Albaret. We find him next in Paris, where from 1791 to 1799 he was the choir conductor at the Feydeau Theater. In 1793 and 1794 he was a member of the Garde Nationale, when he composed his *Hymn* for band. In 1798 he became the professor of solfege at the Conservatory of Music in Paris and from 1798 to 1800 served as the choir conductor (*chef de chant*) at the Opera.

W. 10, Adrien, *Hymne à la Victoire, sur l'évacuation du territoire*

Ou sont ils   ces rois fu - ri-eux   De qui la su-per-be

Poet
  Lacombe

Original instrumentation
  Bass singer, four-part chorus, 2 small and large flutes, 2 oboes, 2 clarinets, 2 trumpets in F, 2 horns in F, trombone, 2 bassoons, serpent, string bass, timpani and *tambour turc* (bass drum)

Documented performance
  October 21, 1794, as part of a ceremony in honor of the French armies of Jourdan and Pichegru over the Duke of York.

Source
  D-TROb, Mss parts, *Musique nationale*, paquet 12 (Pierre)

Commentary
  This composition begins with a rather noble Bass solo, followed by a refrain based on material from the solo. The composition has life and is above average in quality. On September 21, 1794, there was a performance in the Tuileries Garden of a *Hymne à la Fraternité* for choir and "orchestra" composed by, and conducted by, Adrien. It is likely that this work was for band, and not orchestra, but since the music is lost and there is no further information about the performance, one cannot say.

Henri Montan Berton (1767–1844)

BERTON BEGAN HIS STUDY OF MUSIC at age six and by a teenager was playing violin in the orchestra of the Paris Opera. He composed nearly thirty operas but none of them were produced beyond his lifetime. Berton became the choir conductor at the Paris Opera from 1810 to 1815 and after the death of Méhul was awarded his composition class at the Paris Conservatory, where he taught until his death. At this time he wrote two books, a *Methods sur l'Harmonie* and a dictionary of ornaments (*Dictionnaire sur les agreements*) which were very well received. Later he was appointed music director at the Opéra-Italian and there was responsible for bringing to the stage for the first time in Paris Mozart's *Nozze di Figaro*.

As a very conservative member of the Conservatory, Berton played a role in frustrating young Berlioz in his first attempts to win the *Prix de Rome*. Berton is quoted as strongly protesting, "An academy could not and should not encourage a genre of music such as his."

W. 11, Berton, *Marche militaire*

Original instrumentation
2 small and large flutes, 2 clarinets, trumpet in F, 2 horns in F, 2 bassoons, serpent

Source

- F-Pn, printed parts, *Magasin de musique,* Issue 12, Nr. 3
- F-Pn, *Musique Nationale* H2. 12, 3, c. 1795
- D-TROb, Archiv-Nr. Whitwell 0638

Commentary
This march has no particular melodic or harmonic interest.

W. 12, Berton, *Hymne pour la fête de l'Agriculture*

Hommage, hom - ma - ge, hommage, hom - ma - ge

Poet
Lebrun

Original instrumentation
Solo with four-voice chorus (dessus, haute-contre, taille, basse), 2 small flutes, 2 clarinets, 2 trumpets in F, 2 horns in F, 3 trombones, 2 bassoons, serpent, timpani, triangle, *tambour turc* (bass drum)

Documented performance
Festival of Agriculture, June 28, 1796, in Paris.

Source

- F-Pn, printed score by the Conservatory, 1796: *Hymnes de la Revolution*, H2.35, Nr. 11. Another copy: D.16082
- D-TROb, Archiv-Nr. Whitwell 0549

Commentary
This Hymn seems "tongue-in-cheek" in character, something the poet, Lebrun, objected to in a letter quoted above. Berton, however, thought enough of his music to use it again in his opera, *Montano et Stephanie,* first performed April 15, 1799.

A fine, funny and lengthy work which is very worthy of modern performance. The refrain has a percussion introduction, which is very rare in this repertoire.

Matthieu Frédéric Blasius (1758–1829)

BLASIUS WAS BORN OF GERMAN PARENTS in Lauterbourg, France, a town which since the time of Louis XIV had a large military presence and from members of whom he had his first lessons. His brothers Johann Peter, a violinist, and Franz Ignaz, a bassoonist, were also professional musicians in Paris.

Blasius first worked in Strasbourg, for the bishop and for the leader of the civic music, Franz Xaver Richter, co-founder of the "Mannheim School." Moving to Paris in 1788, Blasius became extensively engaged as both violinist and conductor in the theaters and operas, where his work was highly praised.

In 1795 he was appointed as a professor of violin in the new Paris Conservatory. From 1793 to 1795 he was a conductor of the National Guard band and in 1799 became conductor of the bands of the Garde Consulaire. Having lost this position in 1804 be became conductor of the Grenadiers de la Garde de Napoléon. His career as a military conductor continued on under Louis XVIII.

In addition to his *Overture* for band, which follows, the following compositions can also be found in F-Pn:

- *Concerto* for clarinet (Paris: Cochet). Vm 7.10, 526.
- *Method for clarinet* (Paris: Porthaux). L. 9954.
- (6) *Sonatas*, Op. 57, for bassoon and cello (Paris: *Magasin de musique*). Vmg.14903.
- *Suite d'Harmonie* (Paris: Imbault) for pairs of clarinets, horns and bassoons. This is music of a concert nature, not military, and the library has two additional sets under Vm 7.10,530 and Vm 7.10532.
- *Symphonie Concertante* for 2 horns and orchestra. A.33440.

W. 13, Blasius, *Ouverture*

Original instrumentation

2 flutes, 2 oboes, 2 clarinets, 2 trumpets in F, 2 horns in F, 3 trombones, 2 bassoons, serpent.

Sources

- F-Pn, printed parts, H2.8, 1 (*Magasin de musique,* Issue 8, Nr. 1. c/ 1794) with additional copies under H2.125 a-n and D.664
- Dudley, II, 53-73
- D-TROb, Archiv-Nr. Whitwell 0620

Commentary

An uneven work, although not without some interesting features, such as a unison *pp* first theme. It lacks good melodic structure and the harmonic design is too predictable.

Giuseppe Cambini (1746–1825)

CAMBINI WAS BORN IN ITALY, although Mozart referred to him as Swiss-French. According to an early French authority, Cambini and his sweetheart were captured by corsairs and both sold as slaves in Barbary. A wealthy Venetian merchant is said to have bought them in Spain and set them free.

Arriving in Paris, c. 1770, he became very active as a violinist and composer of hundreds of compositions, including some 100 string quartets. He was also an early composer of wind quintets. During the French Revolution he wrote a number of patriotic works but soon began to have health problems and ended his career as a music journalist.

W. 14, Cambini, *Le pas de charge républicain*

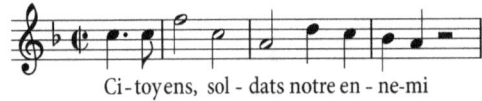
Ci-toyens, sol - dats notre en - ne-mi

Poet
Unknown

Original instrumentation
SSATB chorus, 2 clarinets, 2 trumpets in F, 2 horns in F, bassoons, serpent, tambour

Documented performance
We know only that this work, "to the defenders of the country," was announced in a local newspaper on April 6, 1794.

Source
F-Pn, printed parts (Paris: Boyer), Vm 7 7081

Commentary
This work is in a simple hymn style and a note on one of the parts reads, "can be sung in unison for a nice effect." The tambour part carries the notation, "battant toujours le Pas de Charges," but they are not written out. None of the Cambini compositions listed here are recommended for modern performance.

W. 15, Cambini, *Hymn to the Supreme Being*

ord re é-ter-nel, é-qui-libre im-mu-a-ble

Poet

Unknown

Original instrumentation

Solo voice, 2 oboes or clarinets, 2 horns in F, bassoons, trombone (although the printed part reads "tromboni"

Documented performance

- Festival of the Supreme Being, June 8, 1794
- Music for the Funeral of Marat, September 21, 1794

Source

F-Pn, printed parts (Paris: Boyer), Vm 7 7064

Commentary

The upper woodwinds double the voice throughout. The parts were printed in a small "march book" format.

W. 16, Cambini, *Hymn to the Supreme Being*

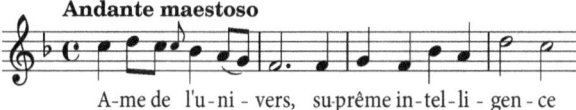

A-me de l'u-ni-vers, su-prême in-tel-li-gen-ce

Poet

Unknown

Original instrumentation

Solo voice, 2 oboes or clarinets, 2 horns in F, bassoons, trombones, serpents and organ

Documented performance

Festival of the Supreme Being, June 8, 1794

Source

F-Pn, printed parts (Paris: Imbault), Vm 7 7056

Commentary

The upper woodwinds double the voice throughout. The wind parts appear to be only a realization of the organ part.

W. 17, Cambini, *Ode to the Victory of Fleurus*

Poet
Unknown

Original instrumentation
Solo voice, 2 oboes or clarinets, 2 horns in F, bassoons, trombones

Documented performance
Victory Celebration, Tuileries, June 29, 1794

Source
F-Pn, printed parts (Paris: Boyer), Vm 7 7065

Commentary
This composition is only a brief march with added words in nine verses.

W. 18, Cambini, *Hymn to Victory*

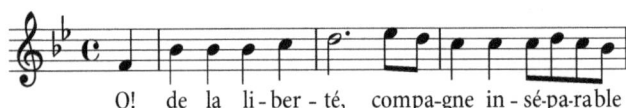

Poet
Unknown

Original instrumentation
Solo voice, 2 oboes or clarinets, bassoons, trombones and "serpentoni"

Documented performance
Probably the Victory Celebration of June 29, 1794

Source
F-Pn, printed parts (Paris: Imbault), Vm 7 7061

Commentary
This is "Nr. 2" of the Imbault series of 1794. The band parts are independent but only serve as accompaniment.

W. 19, Cambini, *Ode on the Two Young Heroes, Barra and Viala*

Peuple, ces deux hé - ros   morts pour la Ré - publi - que

Poet
Unknown

Original instrumentation
Solo voice, 2 clarinets, 2 horns in F, bassoon, trombones and "Basse"

Documented performance
Intended for a ceremony on June 18, 1794

Source
F-Pn, printed parts (Paris: Imbault), Vm 7 7063

Commentary
Intended for a festival in honor of two teenage heroes of the revolution, political chaos caused the ceremony never to be held. Except for the introduction and final cadence the band only doubles the vocal part.

W. 20, Cambini, *Hymn to Virtue*

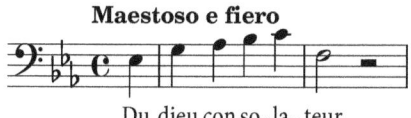

Du dieu con-so-la-teur

Poet
Unknown

Original instrumentation
Solo voice, 2 oboes, 2 clarinets (doubling the oboes), 2 horns in Eb, bassoons, trombones and organ

Documented performance
Unknown

Source
F-Pn, printed parts (Paris: Imbault), Vm 7 7057

Commentary
Basically a march with words added, this is Nr. 7 in the Imbault series of 1794.

W. 21, Cambini, *Hymn to Liberty*

Fière et su-bli-me li-ber-té

Poet
Unknown

Original instrumentation
Solo voice, 2 oboes or clarinets, 2 horns in F, bassoons, trombones, serpents and organ

Documented performance
Unknown

Source
F-Pn, printed parts (Paris: Imbault), Vm 7 7058

Commentary
Nr. 8 in the Imbault series and one of the better examples of that collection. Again, sounds like a march with words added.

W. 22, Cambini, *Hymn to Equality*

Don pré-ci-eux de la na-tu-re, Charme du jus-te

Poet
Unknown

Original instrumentation
Solo voice, 2 oboes or clarinets, 2 horns in F, bassoon, trombones, serpents and organ

Documented performance
Unknown

Source
F-Pn, printed parts (Paris: Imbault), Vm 7 7059

Commentary
This is Nr. 4, and one of the better examples of, the Imbault series.

W. 23, Cambini, *Hymn to the Supreme Being*

La France é - tait la nour-ri-clé-re des grands des prêtres

Poet
Unknown

Original instrumentation
Solo voice, clarinets in C, 2 horns in C, 2 bassoons, serpents, "Bass"

Documented performance
Unknown

Source
F-Pn, printed parts (Paris: Imbault), Vm 7 7062

Commentary
Nr. 5 in the Imbault series, with the publisher mistakenly omitting the final 8 bars of the serpent part.

W. 24, Cambini, *Ode on the Victories*

l'airain bel-li queux a son - né le désespoir

Poet
Arnault

Original instrumentation
Solo voice, 2 clarinets in C, 2 horns in C, 2 bassoons, trombones, "serpentoni," and "Basso"

Documented performance
Unknown

Source
F-Pn, printed parts (Paris: Imbault), Vm 7 7060

Commentary
This is the first and best of the Imbault series, although the winds mostly double the voice.

Charles-Simon Catel (1773–1830)

CHARLES SIMON CATEL was highly respected as a young protégé of Gossec and joined him in writing many compositions for band during the French Revolution. He served as Gossec's assistant with the Guard Band already in 1790.

After the Napoleonic period he became a leading professor of harmony in the Conservatory, where a text he published in 1802 was for many years the leading text on the subject of harmony and formed the foundation of neoclassicism thinking. Berlioz, in his autobiography, wrote of his studying this treatise as he was trying to educate himself in composition. When later a student in the Conservatory, of course, Catel was one of those who disapproved of his music. In 1828 Berlioz describes the elder Catel as being only interested in his roses. Among Catel's other students at the Conservatory were Méhul and the harpist, Charles-Nicolas Bochsa.

In addition to Catel's band works listed below, there are a few interesting chamber works for winds to be found in the national library in Paris:

- (3) *Quartets,* for flute, oboe, English horn and bassoon (Paris: l'Imprimerie du Conservatoire de Music). F-Pn, Cons. A. 35.444
- (3) *Grand Quartets* for flute, oboe, English horn and bassoon. F-Pn, L. 2547
- (3) *Quartets* for clarinet and strings. F-Pn, 35.445.

W. 25, Catel, *Ouverture*

Original instrumentation
2 small flutes, 2 clarinets in C, 2 horns in C, 2 trumpets in C, bass trombone, 2 bassoons, serpent and timpani

Documented performance
- Festival of the Worship of Reason, November 10, 1793
- Concert in Paris, November 20, 1793

Source
- F-Pn, printed parts (*Magasin de musique,* Issue 1, Nr. 1) *Musique Nationale* H2. 1, 1. Another copy under Vm 7 7019
- D-TROb, Archiv-Nr. Whitwell 0616. Piano score and copy of original parts.
- Swanzy, score, 190–212
- Modern edition, Richard F. Goldman as *Overture in C* (Mercury Music)

Commentary
The *Journal de Paris,* in its review of the concert, found this work to be an "absolutely new character. Its results are terrific." I agree, this is a major inspired work which is recommended for modern performance. It begins with an interesting introduction in C minor, followed by two very soft themes. Much instrumental color and harmonic interest, such as the unprepared major key modulations from C to Ab and from G to Eb.

W. 26, Catel, *Ouverture*

Original instrumentation

2 small flutes, 2 clarinets in C, 2 horns in C, 2 trumpets in C, 3 trombone, 2 bassoons, serpent and timpani

Documented performance

- The Celebration of Victories, June 29, 1794
- Concert in Paris, November 7, 1794

Source

- F-Pn, printed parts (*Magasin de musique,* Issue 10, Nr. 1) *Musique Nationale* H2. 10, 1.
- D-TROb, Archiv-Nr. Whitwell 0621. Piano score and copy of original parts.
- Dudley, score in II, 72–108
- Modern edition, Richard F. Goldman as *Overture in F* (Mercury Music)

Commentary

The *Affiches, annonces* Nr. 69, November 19, 1794, notes that this work "excited the just enthusiasm of the audience." I agree, this is a very interesting composition and one of the most adventuresome compositions, harmonically, in this repertoire. Technically, especially in the clarinet part, this is also one of the more difficult works.

W. 27, Catel, *Symphonie*

Original instrumentation

2 small flutes, 2 clarinets, 2 horns, 2 trumpets, 3 trombones, 2 bassoons, serpent, bass drum and timpani

Documented performance

Unknown

Source

F-Pn, printed parts (*Magasin de musique,* Issue 14) *Musique Nationale* H2. 127 a-q. Also, H2. 127 aa-pp

Commentary

This work has a certain lyrical style but there is little interest in the individual melodies or harmony.

W. 28, Catel, *Symphonie militaire*

Original instrumentation

2 small flutes, 2 clarinets, 2 horns in F, 2 trumpets in F, bass trombone, 2 bassoons, serpent, cymbals and bass drum

Documented performance

Unknown

Source

- F-Pn, printed parts (*Magasin de musique,* Issue 5, Nr. 1) *Musique Nationale* H2.5, 1. Another copy under Vm 7 7043
- F-Pn, mss parts, H2.128 a-l *Musique Nationale*
- D-TROb, Archiv-Nr. Whitwell 0614. Piano score and copy of original parts.
- Dudley, score in II, 49-52
- Modern edition, Douglas Townsend (Atlantic Music Supply)

Commentary

Only the second theme seems inspired; the rest is of little interest.

W. 29, Catel, *Marche militaire*

Original instrumentation
Small flute, 2 clarinets, 2 horns in F, 2 trumpets in E, 2 bassoons, serpent, cymbals and bass drum

Documented performance
July 16, 1791

Source
- F-Pn, printed parts (*Magasin de musique,* Issue 1, Nr. 3) *Musique Nationale* H2.1, 3.
- D-TROb, Archiv-Nr. Whitwell 0625. Piano score and copy of original parts.
- Swanzy, score, 213-219 [a reproduction of a score in F-Pn, Bibl. Conservatory 743]

Commentary
A disjunct work with no consistent style.

W. 30, Catel, *Pas de manoeuvre*

Original bnstrumentation
2 small flutes, 2 clarinets in C, 2 horns in F, 2 trumpets in F, 2 bassoons and serpent

Documented performance
Unknown

Source
- F-Pn, printed parts (*Magasin de musique,* Issue 1, Nr. 4) *Musique Nationale* H2.1, 4. Another copy under Vm 7 7022.
- D-TROb, Archiv-Nr. Whitwell 0639. Piano score and copy of original parts.

Commentary
Some charm, but probably not worth modern performance.

W. 31, Catel, *Marche militaire*

Original instrumentation
2 small flutes, 2 clarinets, 2 horns in F, 2 trumpets in F, 2 bassoons and serpent

Documented performance
Unknown

Source

- F-Pn, printed parts (*Magasin de musique,* Issue 3, Nr. 3) *Musique Nationale* H2.3, 3. Another copy under Vm 7 7033.
- D-TROb, Archiv-Nr. Whitwell 0628. Piano score and copy of original parts.

Commentary
Too repetitive to be of interest.

W. 32, Catel, *Marche militaire*

Original instrumentation
2 small flutes, 2 clarinets, 2 horns in F, 2 trumpets in F, 2 bassoons and serpent

Documented performance
Unknown

Source

- F-Pn, printed parts (*Magasin de musique,* Issue 4, Nr. 4) *Musique Nationale* H2.4, 4. Another copy under Vm 7 7040.
- D-TROb, Archiv-Nr. Whitwell 0629. Piano score and copy of original parts.

Commentary
This seems a hastily composed work of little interest. Bars 5–8 are directly borrowed from Gossec's famous *Te Deum*, w. 78.

W. 33, Catel, *Marche militaire*

Original instrumentation
2 small flutes, 2 clarinets in C, 2 horns in F, 2 trumpets in F, 2 bassoons and serpent

Documented performance
Unknown

Source
- F-Pn, printed parts (*Magasin de musique,* Issue 5, Nr. 3) *Musique Nationale* H2.5, 3. Another copy under Vm 7 7045.
- D-TROb, Archiv-Nr. Whitwell 0630. Piano score and copy of original parts.

Commentary
This is one of the best of Catel's marches, a worthy example of the genre.

W. 34, Catel, *Marche militaire*

Original instrumentation
2 small flutes, 2 clarinets, 2 horns in F, trumpet in F, 2 bassoons and serpent

Documented performance
Unknown

Source
- F-Pn, printed parts (*Magasin de musique,* Issue 8, Nr. 3) *Musique Nationale* H2.8, 3.
- D-TROb, Archiv-Nr. Whitwell 0631. Piano score and copy of original parts.

Commentary
This is a march full of pomp, ceremonial in nature, with good variety. A very good, musical march.

W. 35, Catel, *Ode patriotique*

La Sei-ne qui vit son ri - va - que char-gé

Poet

Lebrun

Original instrumentation

Three-part male chorus, 2 flutes, 2 clarinets in C, 2 horns in C, trumpet in C, 2 bassoons, 3 trombones, *tuba curva,* timpani and serpent

Documented performance

- Festival of the Worship of Reason, November 10, 1793
- Concert in Paris, November 20, 1793
- Concert in Paris, November 7, 1794

Source

F-Pn, printed parts, missing 3rd trombone, *Musique Nationale,* paquet 46 (Pierre)

Commentary

This is Catel's first major composition for the Revoluton, composed at age twenty. The *Journal de Paris* wrote after the first concert performance,

> We noticed how pleasing the accompaniment of all the wind instruments is for the listeners; its sound, which is similar to the sound of the voices themselves, makes the harmony parts easier to hear.

This is a three-movement composition, each is substantial but with weak melodic development. The first movement seems to create an atmosphere of calm, but is the least effective of the three. The second movement is dramatic and energetic and the third happy, victorious and heroic.

W. 36, Catel, *Ode sur le vaisseau "le Vengeur"*

Au sommet gla-cé de Rho-do - pe Qui'il

Poet
Lebrun

Original instrumentation
Bass solo, 2 clarinets, 2 horns and 2 bassoons

Documented performance
Unknown

Source
F-Pn, printed parts, (*Collection Époques*) *Hymnes de la Révoluton Française*, H2.15, Nr. 26.

Commentary
This work was apparently composed in the Spring of 1795, although no performance at this time can be documented. The music celebrates an episode in the naval war between the French ship, *le Vengeur* and the British, *Brunswick,* in the Summer of 1794. The two ships drew aside and locked together with their anchors and began firing at point blank range. After a truly heroic effort the French ship sank. Barrère saw this as an opportunity to create some patriotic fervor among the public, whose spirits were a bit low at this time. Thus he gave a very colorful account of the incident in the Convention, picturing the dying French sailors as crying, "Vive la République!" As a result, the public in Paris was for a time quite taken with this battle.

This really is quite a beautiful composition, even though quite simple. The harmonic conception is its central feature, the melody being only a manifestation of the harmony.

W. 37, Catel, *Hymne à l'Être suprême*

Poet
M.-J. Chénier

Original instrumentation
Bass solo, 2 clarinets, 2 horns and 2 bassoons

Documented performance
Unknown

Source
F-Pn, printed parts, (*Collection Époques*) *Hymnes de la Révoluton Française*, H2.15, Nr. 23.

Commentary
This work is based on a text by Chénier which Robespierre would not permit being used in the Festival of the Supreme Being, as Chénier, as former Girondin, was out of favor. As this music appears only in the *Collection Époques* it might have been composed later solely to preserve the words. It is a brief work, but certainly not without expression.

W. 38, Catel, *Hymne à la victoire sur la bataille de Fleurus*

C'est en vain que le Nord en - fan - te

Poet

Lebrun

Original instrumentation

Solo voice, 2 flutes, 2 clarinets, 2 horns in C, 2 trumpets in C, and 2 bassoons, serpent and bass trombone

Documented performance

- June 29 and July 4, 1794
- August 10, 1794, in a now lost version for chorus

Source

- F-Pn, printed parts, (*Magasin de musique,* Issue 5, Nr. 5), *Musique Nationale* H2.5, 5. Additional copies under Vm 7 7047 and 16773.
- D-TROb, Archiv-Nr. Whitwell 0557. Piano score and copy of original parts.
- F-Pn, printed parts (*Collection Époques*) for solo voice, 2 clarinets, 2 horns and 2 bassoons. *Hymnes de la Révolution Française,* H2.15, Nr. 27.

Commentary

This is one of two compositions by Catel based on extracts of Lebrun's "Patriotic Ode." This work is a one-movement composition, brief and simple, which may have been completed and sung on the same day. The work begins with a very strong character, marked *Fiérement,* with a good melodic contour. Oddly, half-way through it seems to lose its conviction and becomes rather weak.

W. 39, Catel, *La bataille des Fleurus*

Non, non, non, non il n'est rien d'impossi - ble

Poet

Lebrun

Original instrumentation

Three-part male chorus, 2 small flutes, 2 clarinets, 2 horns in F, 2 trumpets in C and D, 2 bassoons, 3 trombones, serpent and timpani. We have given above a copyist's invoice for making parts for a total of 50 singers and a band of 63 players.

Documented performance

- Celebrations for the Victories, June 29, 1794 [incomplete]
- Fall of the Bastille, July 14, 1794 [complete]

Source

- F-Pn, printed parts (*Magasin de musique,* Issue 7, Nr. 2) *Musique Nationale* H2.7, 2, and H2.8,2.
- D-TROb, Archiv-Nr. Whitwell 0558. Piano score and copy of original parts.

Commentary

This work remains as a three-movement composition. Later a fourth movement, consisting of a repetition of the first movement with new words was attempted and rejected, as was a fourth movement with original music. The *Magasin de musique,* for reasons which are unknown, apparently published the first two movements only in Issue 7 and then the third movement in Issue 8, under the title, *Suite de la Bataille de Fleurus.*

Here we find one of the best and most inspired of all the band and choral works and certainly one of the best by Catel. The first movement, "très animé," has interesting chromatic harmony and some unison recitative-like choral moments. The second movement, "Modérément," has nice use of dynamics for expressive purposes, and indeed the first horn part carries a note, "Coeur à demi voix." The third movement is a long and interesting "Grave-Allegretto." This movement is more polyphonic that the first two, with independent and difficult wind parts.

W. 40, Catel, *Hymn to Liberty*

De chê-ne et de lau-rier, ceints ta super-be tê - te

Poet

Désorgues

Original instrumentation

Unknown, surviving form in the *Collection Époques* is for solo voice, 2 clarinets, 2 horns and 2 bassoons

Documented performance

Fall of the Bastille, July 14, 1794

Source

- F-Pn, printed parts (*Collection Époques*) *Hymnes de la Révolution Française* H2.15, Nr. 7
- US-DW, an anonymous *Hymn à la Liberte* for voices and piano, US-DW 601

Commentary

The composer's name is not given in any of the surviving sources. It is my belief that this work is by Catel, on the basis of his quotation in bars 5–8 of the unusual harmonic idea first expressed in Gossec's *Te Deum,* in bars 78–81. Catel has quoted this very passage in both his *Marche,* w. 32, and his *Hymn to the Sovereignty of the People,* w. 44. As Catel was a student of Gossec, and no doubt knew the famous *Te Deum,* and as Gossec himself never used this figure again, we believe Catel is here following a pattern which reveals his identity.

The composition appears hastily composed, is brief and without inspiration.

W. 41, Catel, *Ode on the Situation of the Republic during the tyrannie décemvirale*

O vaisseau de l'E-tat fais un dernier ef-fort

Poet
M.-J. Chénier

Original instrumentation
Solo voice, 2 clarinets, 2 horns and 2 bassoons

Documented performance
Perhaps the Ceremony in Honor of the Girondins, Fall, 1793

Source
F-Pn, printed parts (*Collection Époques*) *Hymnes de la Révoluton Française* H2.15, Nr. 29.

Commentary
This work appears to have been conceived for piano accompaniment, not originally for band. While there is some interesting chromatic modulations, the work is not worth modern performance.

W. 42, Catel, *Hymn for August 10*

Jeunes guerre-ers, troupe immor-tel - le

Poet

M.-J. Chénier

Original instrumentation

Four-voice chorus, 2 small flutes, 2 clarinets in C, 2 trumpets in C, 2 horns in C, 3 trombones, 2 bassoons, serpent, *tuba curva, buccin,* timpani, bass drum, cymbals

Documented performance

Celebration of August Tenth (fall of the monarchy), 1795

Source

- F-Pn, printed parts (*Magasin de musique,* Issue 16) *Musique Nationale* H2.35, Nr. 9.
- D-TROb, Archiv-Nr. Whitwell 0510. Piano score and copy of original parts.
- F-Pn, printed parts (*Collection Époques*) for chorus, 2 clarinets, 2 horns and 2 bassoons. *Hymnes de la Révolution Française,* H2.15, Nr. 9.

Commentary

The first movement begins with an unusually long, gloomy introduction, followed by 16 bars of solo, then a refrain for full chorus in a simple hymn style. The second and third movements are harmonized versions of the original material, with differing accompaniments. The fourth movement begins with an introduction again. All in all this is a lengthy and better than average composition in this repertoire.

W. 43, Catel, *Hymn for the Republican banquet for the Festival of Victory*

O jour-dé temel-le me mor-re Em-bel-lis

Poet

Lebrun

Original instrumentation

Solo voice, mixed chorus, 2, flutes or oboes, 2 clarinets in C, 2 trumpets in C, 2 horns in C, 3 trombones, 2 bassoons, serpent and timpani

Documented performance

May 29, 1796

Source

- F-Pn, mss parts, *Musique Nationale* H2.95 a-g
- F-Pn, printed parts, (*Collection Époques*) for chorus, 2 clarinets, 2 horns and 2 bassoons. *Hymnes de la Révolution Française*, H2.15, Nr. 36.

Commentary

The text has current references to the battle of Marengo and the Italian wars. Lebrun's poem carries a quotation from Horace, "Nunc est bibendum nunc pede libero pulsanda tellus." A local newspaper, the *Décade philosophique*, found this very appropriate:

> This ode seems to us to have a double merit; it brings together the consecration of great events in a style as rapid as their succession, it gives life again to the particular genre of d'Alcee and Horace.

We regard this as not one of Catel's better works and not worthy of modern performance.

W. 44, Catel, *Hymn for the Sovereignty of the People*

Sa - lut é-poque sol-en - nel - le

Poet
Lebrun

Original instrumentation
Unknown

Documented performance
March 20, 1799

Source
F-Pn, printed parts (*Collection Époques*) for solo voice, 2 clarinets, 2 horns and 2 bassoons. *Hymnes de la Révolution Française,* H2.15, Livre second, Nr. 3.

Commentary
This is a short, but not a bad work. Still, probably not worth modern performance in my opinion. The composition quotes a passage from the Gossec *Te Deum,* which is also quoted by Catel in his *Marche,* w. 32.

Luigi Cherubini (1760–1842)

CHERUBINI BEGAN MUSIC STUDY at age six and had composed several religious works by age thirteen and thirteen operas by age twenty-eight. After a period of study and travel he settled in Paris for the rest of his life. His early composition centered in opera and he had a major success in 1791 with *Lodoïska*. His somewhat grim and serious nature caused him difficulties during the period of the French Revolution and after, although Napoleon extended several honors to him. His works were frequently praised by Haydn, Beethoven (who regarded Cherubini as the greatest of his contemporaries), Schumann and Brahms, in whose music studio upon his death the only picture of any composer was an engraving of Cherubini.

As an older man Cherubini became, in 1822, the director of the Conservatory in Paris, where his role was often criticized by the young Berlioz. Though he remained unpopular with some due to his personal irritability, he nevertheless had important friends, such as Rossini and Chopin.

In addition to the large scale works discussed below, Cherubini also wrote a considerable number of marches. In D-TROb one can find copies of these which I collected.

- *March* from the Opera, *Die Tage der Gefahr (Les deux journées)* for 222-02 and contrabassoon, dated October 4, 1805, at Hetzendorf, while Cherubini was briefly head of music in Vienna. Archiv-Nr. Whitwell 0056

- *Eight Marches,* edited by Karl Hass for 5 brass (New York: Mills Music, Nr. 867, c. 1962). Archiv-Nr. Whitwell 0397

- *Marcia,* for band, composed for Barone di Braun in Vienna, 1805. Archiv-Nr. Whitwell 0785.

- *Marcia in F* for band (Milano: Istituto Internazionale "Luigi Cherubini," c. 1983). Archiv-Nr. Whitwell 0448

W. 45, Cherubini, *Hymn to the Panthéon*

Poet

M.-J. Chénier

Original Instrumentation

Three-part male chorus, 2 small flutes, 2 clarinets, 2 trumpets in C, 2 horns in F, 3 trombones, 2 bassoons, serpent, timpani, gong and bass drum

Documented performance

Festival of the Fifth Sans-culottide, September 21, 1794, when a copyist's invoice reflects a band of 68 players.

Source

- F-Pn, printed parts (*Magasin de musique,* Issue 12, Nr. 2) for chorus, 2 clarinets, 2 horns and 2 bassoons. *Hymnes de la Révolution Française* H2.12, Nr. 2.
- D-TROb Archiv Nr. Whitwell 0578, a copy of the above.

Commentary

This is a very long composition in three movements of through-composed style. One hears echoes here of the famous Gossec *Marche lugubre,* w. 73, with exposed timpani and gong parts. The wind parts are very independent, beginning with a very expressive horn and clarinet dialog. There are rich harmonic moments and interesting chromaticism throughout. This is one of the most interesting and musical compositions in the entire Revolutionary repertoire.

W. 46, Cherubini, *Hymn to Fraternity*

Nous a - vons chanté   la vic-toire   A nos coeurs don-nous

Poet

Désorgues

Original Instrumentation

Four-part male chorus, 2 small flutes, 2 clarinets, 2 trumpets in C, 4 horns in F and Bb, 2 bassoons, serpent, timpani, gong and bass drum, *tambour turc*

Documented performance

Festival of the Fifth Sans-culottide, September 21, 1794, when a copyist's invoice reflects a band of 68 players.

Source

- Mss score, Nr. 116 (2) Catalog Bottée de Toulmon, Prussian National Library, Berlin
- F-Pn, printed parts (*Collection Époques*) for solo voice, 2 clarinets, 2 horns and 2 bassoons. *Hymnes de la Révolution Française* H2.15, Nr. 31.

Commentary

The Committee of Public Instruction ordered 18,000 copies of this work in a version for solo singer and "basse," to be handed out to the armies. For us, this work seems to lack inspiration and was perhaps composed in a hurry.

W. 47, Cherubini, *Hymn for August 10*

S'il en est qui veu-lent un maî - tre s'il est des coeurs

Poet

Lebrun

Original Instrumentation

Four-part male chorus, 2 small flutes, 2 clarinets, 2 trumpets in C, 2 horns in C, 3 trombones, 2 bassoons, serpent, *buccin, tuba curva,* cymbals and bass drum

Documented performance

Celebration of August Tenth (fall of the monarchy), 1793

Source

- F-Pn, Bibl. Cons., 10948, autograph score (Pierre)
- Mss score, Nr. 116 (3) Catalog Bottée de Toulmon, Prussian National Library, Berlin
- F-Pn, printed parts (*Collection Époques*) for solo voice, 2 clarinets, 2 horns and 2 bassoons. *Hymnes de la Révolution Française* H2.15, Nr. 15.
- F-Pn, mss parts, Bibl. Cons., *Musique nationale,* paquet 16 (Pierre). H2.31

Commentary

The newspaper, *Decade philosophique* for September 6, 1795, had high praise for his poem by Lebrun.

> On seeing the ten verses he has recently added one will be struck by the warmth of the whole of this new and bold composition. It is half in the style of Pindar and half in the style of Alcee, the only one of the lyric poets who had the glory to brave the tyrants, to combat with song their defeat.

The paper went on to contend that Cherubini had not done justice to this poem. We agree; it is uninspired and lacks melodic interest.

W. 48, Cherubini, *Hymn for August 10*

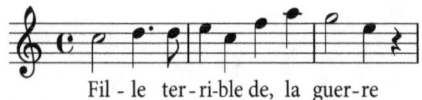
Fil - le ter - ri - ble de, la guer - re

Documented performance

Carbon de Flins

Original instrumentation

Solo voice, 2 small flutes, 2 clarinets in C, 2 trumpets in C, 2 horns in C, 3 trombones, 2 bassoons, serpent, *buccin, tuba curva,* timpani and bass drum

Documented performance

Recognition of Victories, May 29, 1796

Source

- F-Pn, Vm 7 7956, mss score, made by Pierre from parts in the Conservatory
- F-Pn, mss parts, *Musique Nationale* H2.99 a-v
- F-Pn, V 7 m.a.2545, printed choral part (Paris: Leduc, 19th century)

Commentary

A very good example of Cherubini, consisting of solo and refrain in three verses. This composition has an unusually long band introduction of 24 bars.

W. 49, Cherubini, *Funeral Hymn on the Death of General Hoche*

Du haut de la voûtre é - ter - nel   le Jeu - ne-héros

Poet

M.-J. Chénier

Original instrumentation

Solo mixed quartet, three-part male chorus, 2 small flutes, 2 large flutes, 2 clarinets, 2 trumpets in C (with and without mutes), 2 horns in C and Eb, 3 trombones, 2 bassoons, timpani

Documented performance

- Funeral of General Hoche, October 1, 1797
- Funeral of General Joubert, 1799

Source

- Mss score, Nr. 116 (5) Bottée de Toulmon catalog, Prussian National Library, Berlin
- F-Pn, mss parts, *Musique Nationale* H2.34
- F-Pn, *Hymnes de la Révolution Française* H2.15, Nr. 38, *Collection Époques,* version for solo voice, 2 clarinets, 2 horns and 2 bassoons.
- D-TROb, Archiv-Nr. Whitwell, 1378, a copy of the autograph score.

Commentary

Compositions written for dramatic moments such as this one often were repeated in local theaters for the public to hear. In this case, on October 10, 1797, in the Feydeau Street Theater, this work was inserted into a performance of *Romeo.* A local paper, *L'Ami des lois,* observed the following day,

> A touching funeral ceremony consecrated to the memory of General Hoche ... An effect worthy of the dignity and grandeur of the subject.

We find this one of the very best compositions of the French Revolution repertoire. The introduction, with the most haunting percussion, is very striking.

W. 50, Cherubini, *Le Salpêtre républicain*

Descendons dan nos sou-ter rains La li-ber-té nous

Poet

Unknown

Original Instrumentation

Solo voice, 2 clarinets, 2 horns and 2 bassoons

Documented performance

Spring, 1798

Source

- Mss score, Nr. 116 (7) Bottée de Toulmon catalog, Prussian National Library, Berlin
- F-Pn, *Hymnes de la Révolution Française* H2.15, Nr. 21, *Collection Époques,* version for solo voice, 2 clarinets, 2 horns and 2 bassoons.

Commentary

Based on a text of 1794 intended to inspire miners to mine more saltpeter, a substance used in gunpowder. A member of the Directory, Neufchateau, sent a copy of a song from this period to Sarrette in February 1798 asking him to have it reset to music for the *Collection Époques,* then in preparation ("would not the collection admit some gaiety?"). It is short, lighthearted, a popular song in the manner of Gilbert and Sullivan.

W. 51, Cherubini, *Le Salpêtre républicain*

O jour é-ter-nel --le mé moi - re

Poet

Andrieux

Original Instrumentation

Three-part male chorus, 2 small flutes, 2 clarinets in C, 2 trumpets in F, 2 horns in F, 3 trombones, 2 bassoons, serpent, string bass, timpani

Documented performance

Festival of the Sovereignty of the People, September 4, 1796

Source

- F-Pn, Cons., 10948, autograph score, according to Pierre
- F-Pn, mss parts, Bibl. Cons., *Musique Nationale,* paquet 18 (Pierre). Another copy under *Musique Nationale* H2.32
- Mss score, Nr. 116 (6) Bottée de Toulmon catalog, Prussian National Library, Berlin
- F-Pn, *Hymnes de la Révolution Française* H2.15, Nr. 37, *Collection Époques,* version for solo voice, 2 clarinets, 2 horns and 2 bassoons.

Commentary

A lengthy, major work with interesting harmonic adventures, moments of lyricism and even mystery. It contains a firey Allegro spiritoso, followed by a hymn-like choral section. There is much to recommend this composition.

W. 52, Cherubini, *Le Salpêtre républicain*

De l'hi - ver le courroux ex - pi - re

Poet
Parny

Original Instrumentation
Voice with 2 clarinets, 2 horns and 2 bassoons

Documented performance
Festival of the Celebration of Youth, March 30, 1799

Source

- Mss score, Nr. 116 (8) Bottée de Toulmon catalog, Prussian National Library, Berlin
- F-Pn, *Hymnes de la Révolution Française* H2.15 Livre second, Nr. 4, *Collection Époques*

Commentary

This work was requested of Cherubini by the Minister of the Interior on October 20, 1798. The result is a mindless little tune, hardly worthy of Cherubini.

W. 53, Cherubini, *Fête de al Reconnaissance*

Pa - ré de verdure et de fluers   Prairi - al aux

Poet
Mahérault

Original Instrumentation
Voice with 2 clarinets, 2 horns and 2 bassoons

Documented performance
Festival of Recognition, May 29, 1794

Source

- Mss score, Nr. 116 (9) Bottée de Toulmon catalog, Prussian National Library, Berlin
- F-Pn, *Hymnes de la Révolution Française* H2.15 Livre second, Nr. 6, *Collection Époques*

Commentary
Due to an independent wind accompaniment, this is one of the more interesting compositions for voice and six winds.

Nicolas Dalayric (1753–1809)

DALAYRIC WAS EDUCATED AS A LAWYER and, in a rare sequence, was urged by his father to leave law and concentrate on his passion for music. He wrote a great number of operas for the Paris stage, which formed the center of his reputation. In 1804 he received the *Légion d'honneur*.

W. 53 bis, Dalayric, *Les canons*

Poet
Unknown

Original instrumentation
Solo singer, 2 clarinets and bassoon

Source

- F-Pn, *Magasin de musique*
- D-TROb Archiv Nr. Whitwell 0592, a copy of the above.

Commentary

In my collection I also have a copy of a work by this composer for singer and basse, *Adieux d'un a son fils, en l'envoyant aux frontières*, D-TROb Archiv Nr. Whitwell 0657, copy of another publication of the *Magasin de musique*, c. 1795.

François Devienne (1759–1803)

DEVIENNE WAS ONE OF FOURTEEN CHILDREN of a saddle maker and whose early interest in music resulted in the composition of a Mass with wind instruments at age ten. He became much in demand as a flutist, but also played bassoon in the opera orchestra. He became a member of the band of the National Guard and taught in the band's Free School, National Institute of Music and finally in the Conservatory, where he also became an administrator.

While he composed fifteen operas, one very successful, *Les visitandines* (1792), most of his compositions were in the field of wind instruments, including a great many concerti, sonatas and various studies for individual instruments. One of his compositions, his *Symphonie concertant* for flute, oboe, horn and bassoon was featured in the concert of November 20, 1793, by members of the Guard Band. A local newspaper, the *Journal de Paris,* reviewed this performance and observed,

> Never before has Paris presented such a complete gathering of talents of the first order in the field of wind instruments; people have never heard such lovely music with such effectiveness ... The *Symphonie concertante* by Devienne, performed by the composer, Sallantin, F. Duvernoy and Ozi with such perfection that we would not have imagined it within the capabilities of these artists had we not known that anything is possible to artists who do not disdain polishing the gifts of nature by constant practice.

It was perhaps this constant practice, and the dedication it represented, which brought his early death, at age forty-three, in a lunatic asylum at Charenton, near Paris. One early source attributed his death to "the intensity of his professional studies."

W. 54, Devienne, *Ouverture*

Original instrumentation

2 small flutes, 2 oboes, 2 clarinets, 2 trumpets in F, 2 horns in F, trombone, 2 bassoons, serpent, timpani

Documented performance

Performed at a student concert in the Feydeau Theater, May 30, 1794.

Source

- F-Pn, printed parts, *Magasin de musique,* Issue 7, Nr. 1, *Musique Nationale* H2.7, 1
- D-TROb Archiv Nr. Whitwell 0619, a copy of the above.

Commentary

A very uneven work with harmonic progressions which move too slowly, spread across too many bars, and a general lack of lyricism.

W. 55, Devienne, *Hymn to the Eternal*

Poet

Geoffroy

Original instrumentation

Voice, 2 clarinets, 2 horns, 2 bassoons

Documented performance

Unknown

Source

F-Pn, printed parts, *Collection Époques, Hymnes de la Révolution Française* H2.15, Nr. 25

Commentary

The composition seems very labored, including moments of chromatic interest followed by almost banal harmony.

W. 56, Devienne, *Le Chant du rdetour*

La paix couronne la vic-toi - re, Français

Poet

Legrand

Original instrumentation

Solo voice, 2 small flutes, 2 clarinets in C, 2 horns in F, trombone, 2 bassoons, timpani

Documented performance

A reference only dated 31, 1797, by Legrand, historian to the Army of the Rhein.

Source

Believed to be lost.

Frédéric Duvernoy (1765–1838)

DUVERNOY WAS A SELF-TAUGHT HORN PLAYER who gained a European reputation as a player and teacher. His brother, Charles, was a clarinetist in the Opera and his brothers, Rudolf and Jean Auguste, were violinists. A horn player in the orchestra of the Italian Comedy Theater, in 1790 he joined the band of the National Guard. In 1795 he became a faculty member of the Paris Conservatory.

W. 57, Duvernoy, *Pas de manoeuvre*

Original instrumentation
2 small flutes, 2 clarinets, 2 horns in F, trumpet in F, 2 bassoons, serpent

Documented performance
Unknown

Source

- F-Pn, printed parts, *Magasin de musique*, Issue 4, Nr. 5, *Musique Nationale* H2.4, 5. An additional copy is found under Vm 7 7041.
- D-TROb Archiv Nr. Whitwell 0642

Commentary
A nice example of this kind of march form, with a trio in minor.

André-Frédéric Eler (1764–1821)

ELER WAS LONG ASSOCIATED with the Paris Conservatory as a librarian and teacher of accompaniment and solfege. In addition to the works below there are some chamber wind works in F-Pn.

- MS 1929, autograph score, (3) *Quartets* for horn and strings
- MS 1928, (3) *Quartets* for flute, clarinet, horn and bassoon. The same, F-Pn A. 33.900 (Paris: Pleyel)
- A. 33.895, (3) *Quartets* for 2 clarinets, horn and bassoon (Paris: Pleyel).
- MS 1930, (3) *Trios* for flute, clarinet and bassoon.

W. 58, Eler, *Overture*

Original instrumentation
2 small flutes, 2 oboes, 2 clarinets, 2 horns in C, trumpet in C, 2 bassoons, 3 trombones, serpent and timpani

Documented performance
Unknown

Source

- F-Pn, printed parts, *Magasin de musique,* Issue 1: *Hymnes et Symphonies* H2.44, Nr. 16. The parts can be found under *Musique Nationale* H2.130A, a-w and *Musique National* H2.130B, 1-q.
- D-TROb Archiv Nr. Whitwell 0624

Commentary
An aimless composition.

W. 59, Eler, *Ode on the Situation of the Republic in May, 1799*

Quel est ce vaiseau dont les voi - les

Poet
Lebrun

Original instrumentation
Solo voice, 2 clarinets, 2 horns, 2 bassoons

Documented performance
May 29, 1794

Source
F-Pn, printed parts (*Collection Époques*) *Hymnes de la Révolution Française* H2.15, Nr. 41.

Commentary
A nice melodic voice part, but an accompaniment without character.

Abbé Feray

LITTLE IS KNOWN today about the Abbé Feray, music master at the Church of Saint-Roch in 1792.

W. 60, Feray, *Strophes on the Anniversary of the Just Punishment of the Last King of France*

Poet
Desforges

Original instrumentation
Chorus, 2 oboes, 2 clarinets, 2 horns, 2 bassoons

Documented performance
Celebration of January 21, 1795

Source
Believed to be lost.

Commentary
A copyist's invoice for the parts for this out of doors performance was for 38 singers, 12 clarinets, 4 oboes, 6 horns and 6 bassoons.

Georg Friedrich Fuchs (1752–1821)

FUCHS WAS A GERMAN COMPOSER and conductor studied with Haydn and Cannabich. He was the conductor of a military band in Zweibrucken before moving to Paris in 1784. When the Paris Conservatory was founded, he was the first clarinet professor.

In addition to the band works below, one may find the following chamber works by Fuchs in F-Pn.

- MS. 1966, autograph score, *Concerto* for clarinet
- K. 2019 (incomplete set) *Concerto* Nr. 4 for horn (Paris: Naderman)
- Vm 7.1375, (3) *Quartets* for horn and strings (Paris: Imbault)
- Cons. A.34.042, (3) *Quartets* for clarinet, horn, bassoon and cello (Paris: *Magasin de musique*)
- Cons. A.34.041 (3) *Quartets* for clarinet, 2 horns and bassoon (Paris: chez Boyer)
- Vm 9.310 *Bataille d'Austerlitz* for 2 clarinets, also under Vm 9.310 and Vm 9.310a. The same work for two flutes can be found under Vm 9.2157.
- H2.177, *Aria* from Cimarosa's *The Secret Marriage,* arranged by Fuchs for 2 flutes, 2 clarinets and 2 bassoons.
- US-DW 198 In view of the many band arrangements by Fuchs, he may have had something to do with an anonymous eighteenth century band collection, *Les Aires Ordinaires.*

W. 61, Fuchs, *Le Siège de Lille*

Original instrumentation
  4 clarinets, 2 horns, trumpet, 2 bassoons, cymbals, bass drum

Documented performance
  Unknown

Source
  F-Pn, printed parts (Paris: Naderman), believed to be lost

Commentary
  This work is known only through the mention of its publication by the *Chronique de Paris* on November 12, 1792.

W. 62, Fuchs, *Le Siège de Thionville*

Original instrumentation
4 clarinets, 2 horns, trumpet, 2 bassoons, cymbals, bass drum

Documented performance
Unknown

Source
F-Pn, printed parts (Paris: Naderman), believed to be lost.

Commentary
This work is known only through the mention of its publication by the *Affiches* on February 19, 1793.

W. 63, Fuchs, *Le Bataille de Gemmapes et la prise de la ville de Mons*

Original instrumentation
4 clarinets, 2 horns, trumpet, 2 bassoons, cymbals, bass drum

Documented performance
Unknown

Source
F:Pn, printed parts (Paris: Naderman), believed to be lost

Commentary
This work is known only through the mention of its publication by the *Chronique de Paris* on January 14, 1793.

W. 64, Fuchs, as arranger, *Ouverture du Camp de Grand-Pré*

Original instrumentation
Unknown

Documented performance
Unknown

Source
F-Pn, printed parts (Paris: Naderman), believed to be lost.

Commentary
This work is known only through the mention of its publication by the *Chronique de Paris* on April 24, 1794.

W. 65, Fuchs, as arranger, *Airs du Camp de Grand-Pré*

Original instrumentation

4 clarinets, 2 horns, trumpet, 2 bassoons, cymbals, bass drum

Documented performance

Unknown

Source

F-Pn, D.16118, printed parts (Paris: Naderman)

Commentary

The publication of this work dates from Spring 1794 and consists of seven movements, all taken from the works of Gossec.

Dieu de peuple

Vous gentilles fillettes

Les habitans de ces boccages

Dans le temps de notre jeunesse

Qu'une fete ici sapprete

Que devient l'ardeur intrepide

À peine sur ces monts

François Réné Gebauer (1773–1844)

GEBAUER WAS THE SON of a German military musician and had four brothers, all of whom were musicians and composers: Michel-Joseph Gebauer (1763–1812), Pierre-Paul Gebauer, Jean-Luc Gebauer and Etienne-François Gebauer.

François Rene Gebauer was a student of Devienne and performed as a bassoonist with the Swiss Guard in Versailles before joining the National Guard Band in 1790. After the revolutionary period he was active as a bassoonist in the Opera and a professor in the Conservatory.

In addition to his two band works below, in F-Pn one can also find some of his wind chamber works.

- W.24.117, autograph score, *Menuet du Diable* for bassoon
- K. 1848, *Quartet* for bassoon and strings
- L. 2552 (1-4), (3) *Quartets*, Op. 27, for flute, oboe, English horn and bassoon
- L. 2554 (1-6) (3) *Quintets* for flute, clarinet, oboe, horn and bassoon

W. 66, Gebauer, F., *Pas de manoeuvre*

Original instrumentation
2 small flutes, 2 clarinets, trumpet in F, 2 horns in F, 2 bassoons, serpent

Documented performance
Unknown

Source

- F-Pn, printed parts, *Magasin de musique*, Issue 5, Nr. 4: *Musique Nationale* H2.5, 4. Another copy can be found under Vm 7 7046.
- D-TROb Archiv Nr. Whitwell 0643

Commentary
Not an interesting march, except for a minor trio.

W. 67, Gebauer, F., *Pas de manoeuvre*

Original instrumentation

2 small flutes, 2 clarinets, trumpet in F, 2 horns in F, 2 bassoons, serpent

Documented performance

Unknown

Source

- F-Pn, printed parts, *Magasin de musique,* Issue 8, Nr. 4: *Musique Nationale* H2.8, 4.
- D-TROb Archiv Nr. Whitwell 0644

Commentary

Not an interesting march, but perhaps the best by Gebauer.

Michel-Joseph Gebauer (1763–1812)

GEBAUER, A BROTHER TO THE ABOVE, was an oboist in the Swiss Guard at age fourteen and also played the violin and viola. In 1791 he joined the band of the French National Guard and was a professor in the Conservatory. After the revolution he remained a member of the band, now called the Imperial Guard, under Napoleon. He had the misfortune to be one of a great many French musicians who died on the *Grande-Armée's* retreat from Moscow.

W. 68, Gebauer, M.-J., *Pas de manoeuvre*

Original instrumentation
2 small flutes, 2 clarinets, trumpet in F, 2 horns in F, 2 bassoons, serpent

Documented performance
Unknown

Source
- F-Pn, printed parts, *Magasin de musique,* Issue 9, Nr. 4: *Musique Nationale* H2.9, 4.
- D-TROb Archiv Nr. Whitwell 0645

Commentary
A very dull example.

W. 69, Gebauer, M.-J., *Pas de manoeuvre*

Original instrumentation
2 small flutes, 2 clarinets, trumpet in F, 2 horns in F, 2 bassoons, serpent

Documented performance
Unknown

Source
- F-Pn, printed parts, *Magasin de musique,* Issue 9, Nr. 3: *Musique Nationale* H2.9, 3.
- D-TROb Archiv Nr. Whitwell 0637

Commentary
A very dull example.

W. 69bis, Geveaux, *Symphonie concertante*

Original instrumentation
flute, oboe, horn and bassoon

Documented performance
Performed on a student concert, May 30, 1794

Source
Lost

Commentary
An article in the *London Magazine* for 1826, discussing persons who died in 1825, calls Geveaux, "a composer of a very inferior class, but distinguished by grace and lightness."

François-Joseph Gossec (1734–1829)

GOSSEC WAS PERHAPS THE MOST TALENTED French composer in the generation after Rameau and certainly had one of the most remarkable careers. Showing an early talent for music, he went to Paris in 1751 and became a student of Rameau. He followed Rameau as the conductor of a private orchestra belonging to a wealthy businessman, La Poupelinière, who aspired to live like a noble. Next Gossec worked for a real noble, the Prince de Condé. It was at this time that Mozart met him on a trip to Paris and found him to be "a good friend and a very dry man."

Whereas the very nature of the French Revolution, which began in 1789, was anti-monarchy, it caused all who were associated with nobles to fall from favor. It is particularly amazing that Gossec, with his entire career so far associated with nobles, was able to become the leading composer of the revolution and together with Méhul became a conductor of the band of the *Garde Nationale*. He also became one of the administrators of the Paris Conservatory when it was founded in 1795.

Once again, after the revolution, with its strong prejudice within the various political factions, Gossec was able to exit untouched and return to work under the monarchy until he retired.

In addition to the original revolutionary band works listed below, there are some very interesting early Harmoniemusik compositions, all for 2 clarinets, 2 horns and bassoons, written during Gossec's service with the Prince de Condé, 1766–1769. The autograph scores for the last three works are all found in F-Pn, MS 1436. Listed below, with the titles, are the archiv shelf-list numbers for my copies in Trossingen, which may be easier to view than going to Paris.

- *Le Bataille,* autograph parts, Archiv Nr. Whitwell 0266, also in F-Pn MS 1491 a-f
- *La Chasse d'Hyulas et Silvie à Chentilli,* autograph score, Archiv Nr. Whitwell 0270
- *Simphonie à 6,* autograph score, Archiv Nr. Whitwell 0267
- *Piéces pour le prince de Condé,* autograph score, Archiv Nr. Whitwell 0269

W. 70, Gossec, *Symphonie militaire*

Original instrumentation

2 small flutes, 2 oboes, 2 clarinets in C, 2 trumpets in F, 2 horns in F, 2 bassoons, serpent or string bass, timpani and bass drum

Documented performances

Unknown

Source

- F-Pn, *Magasin de musique*, Issue 2, Nr. 1, *Musique Nationale* H2.2, 1, printed parts. Another copy is under Vm 7 7025.
- D-TROb Archiv Nr. Whitwell 0611, a copy of the above.
- Modern editions: Richard F. Goldman (Mercury Music) and William Schaefer (University of Southern California).

Commentary

This Symphony begins in F major, whereas the final movement ends in C major. While this is rare, but not unique, Swanzy in "A Choral Wind Symphony?" (*Journal of Band Research*, VI, Nr. 1, Fall, 1969) contends that the Gossec *Choeur Patriotique,* w. 86, which begins in the key of F, was intended as the final movement because it follows this Symphonie in the *Magasin de musique* series. This is possible, although I have not been able to document the idea, nor even a performance of the Symphonie itself. The latter may be because, in my opinion, this work is uninspired, very dull, and not recommended for modern performance.

W. 71, Gossec, *Symphonie in C*

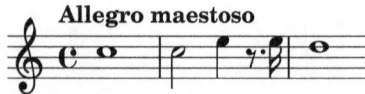

Original instrumentation

2 small flutes, 2 oboes, 2 clarinets, 2 horns in F, 2 bassoons, 3 trombones, serpent, *tuba curva*, *buccin* and timpani

Documented performances

The Celebration of August Tenth, 1794

Source

- F-Pn, Ms score *Musique Nationale* H2.154.
- Modern edition: Richard F. Goldman (Mercury Music)

Commentary

This one-movement composition is excellent, with vitality and interest. This is certainly one of the best of Gossec's instrumental efforts.

W. 72, Gossec, *Concertante*

Original instrumentation

Solo instruments: 2 flutes, 2 oboes, 2 clarinets, 2 horns and bassoon, with an accompaniment of 2 trumpets, bassoon, 3 trombones, contreclarion, and timpani

Documented performances

- Concert of November 20, 1793
- Festival of Reason

Source

F-Pn, Bibl. Cons, *Musique d'hrmonie*, paquet 13 (Pierre). Unfortunately in which all the solo parts, except the oboe, are incomplete, leaving the original instrumentation somewhat in doubt. The *Journal de Paris* (November 21, 1793) reports,

> Symphonie conertante for eleven wind instruments (petite flute, grand flute, clarinette, hautbois, cors, bassons, serpent et contreclairon ... The contreclairon was created by one, Hostie, to "nourish the part of the bass" and that "he still needs to perfect it."

Commentary

There is no question that this is a major lost work, for the first movement consists of 362 bars, followed by a slow movement of nearly 200 bars and a Finale, Theme and Variations. The original review, quoted above, concluded,

> The famous Gossec has added merit to the difficulties he conquered by presenting a composition as melodious as it is full of verve, grand, and harmony.

W. 73, Gossec, *Marche lugubre*

Original instrumentation

2 small flutes, 2 clarinets, 2 trumpets in F, 2 horns in F, 3 trombones, 2 bassoons, serpent, tam-tam, bass drum and *caisse roulante voilee*

Documented performances

- Funeral service for the victims of Nancy, September 20, 1790. The *Journal de la Municipalité,* September 23, 1790, wrote,

    The sharp noise of the tam tam (instrument arabe) combined with cymbals and brass and interrupted by intervals of silence gives to the soul the most sorrowful sensations and inspires a contemplative mood.

- Ceremony for Mirabeau, April 4, 1791, the *Révolutions de Paris,* April, 1791, writing,

    The notes, detached from one another, break the heart, pulling at ones insides.

    The *Moniteur,* April 6, 1791, adds,

    The mournful roll of the drum and the sound of the funeral instruments filled the soul with religious terror.

- The Festival of Law
- The Federation, 1792
- The Funeral of Lazowski

Source

- F-Pn, printed parts (Paris: chez Imbault), missing tam-tam, *Magasin de musique,* Issue 12, Nr. 1, *Musique Nationale* H2.12, 1. Another copy under Musique Nationale H2.143 a-q.
- D-TROb Archiv Nr. Whitwell 0635, a copy of the above
- F-Pn, Bibl. Cons., mss score of 1793, according to Pierre
- F-Pn, Bibl. Cons., *Musique d'harmonie,* paquet 37 (Pierre) a mss tam-tam part.
- Modern edition: Douglas Townsend, as part of *Gossec Suite Nr. 4* (Franco Colombo). A copy can be found in D-TROb Archiv Nr. Whitwell 1567. This is a very usable modern edition, provided one makes the following alterations:
    1. The timpani part, contrary to the indication on the first page, is not original.
    2. Omit the *mf* in bar 10.
    3. In bars 13–14 there should be no diminuendo, only a subito *pp* on the third beat of bar 15.

4. Bar 22 should read *ff*.
5. In bars 26–30 the original had no indicated dynamic level. If anything a crescendo is desired, rather than the published version.
6. Bar 39, all entrances should read *ff*.
7. Bars 45–46. The original has neither *fz* nor an accent.
8. "Cymbal," in this score should read "tam-tam."

Commentary

This march is certainly one of the most interesting and musical compositions of the French Revolutionary repertoire. Most unusual for this time is the almost Wagnerian use of harmony, instead of melody, to carry the emotional impact. There are a very expressive use of dynamics and dramatic unison passages.

The use of the tam-tam, which was new for listeners in Paris, especially in letting the tam-tam ring during ensemble rests, was a dramatic idea copied by later composers, most noticeably in the beginning of the *Hymn funèbre,* w. 49, by Cherubini and in the Funeral Marche of the Bochsa *Requiem for Louis XVI* (1815). Also the beginning melodic idea, with its upper chromatic neighboring-tone, was used in the same Bochsa movement and also in the beginning of the *Symphony for Band* by Reicha (1815).

W. 74, Gossec, *Marche religieuse*

Original instrumentation
2 flutes, 2 clarinets, trumpet in Eb, 2 horns in Eb, 2 bassoons and serpent

Documented performances
Unknown

Source

- F-Pn, printed parts, *Magasin de musique*, Issue 6, Nr. 3, *Musique Nationale* H2.6, 3. Another copy under Vm 7 7050.
- D-TROb Archiv Nr. Whitwell 0626, a copy of the above.

Commentary
A more legato style for a march, but it remains a brief and uninteresting work.

W. 75, Gossec, *Marche funèbre*

Original instrumentation

2 small flutes, 2 clarinets, 2 trumpets in Eb, 2 horns in Eb, 3 trombones, 2 bassoons, serpent, *tuba curva* in Bb, tam-tam and "drum or timpani"

Documented performances

- Concert of November 20, 1793
- Concert of November 7, 1794
- Ceremony on the Death of Gen. Hoche

Source

- F-Pn, printed parts (Paris: Imbault), *Musique Nationale* H2.14.
- D-TROb Archiv Nr. Whitwell 0625, a copy of the above.

Commentary

This is perhaps a sequel to the *Marche*, w. 73, but it lacks the drive and emotional impact. Still, it is unusual and is not without interest.

W. 76, Gossec, *Marche victorieuse*

Original instrumentation

2 small flutes, 2 clarinets, trumpet, 2 horns, 2 bassoons and serpent

Documented performances

Unknown

Source

- F-Pn, printed parts, *Musique Nationale* H2.6 Nr. 4. Another copy is found under Vm 7 7051.
- D-TROb Archiv Nr. Whitwell 0632, a copy of the above.

Commentary

This is one of the best of the marches of Gossec. A real "victory" march, noble and not too busy.

W. 77, Gossec, *Marche*

Original instrumentation

2 small flutes, 2 clarinets, trumpet, 2 horns in F, 2 bassoons and serpent

Documented performances

Unknown

Source

- F-Pn, printed parts, *Magasin de musique,* Issue 10, Nr. 3 *Musique Nationale* H2.10, 3.
- D-TROb Archiv Nr. Whitwell 0634, a copy of the above.

Commentary

This march is of little interest.

W. 78, Gossec, *Marche*

Original instrumentation

2 small flutes, 2 clarinets, trumpet in F, 2 horns in F, 2 bassoons and serpent

Documented performances

Unknown

Source

- F-Pn, printed parts, *Magasin de musique,* Issue 11, Nr. 3 *Musique Nationale* H2.11, 3.
- D-TROb Archiv Nr. Whitwell 0635, a copy of the above.

Commentary

This march is of little interest.

W. 79, Gossec, *Te Deum*

Te De - um lau - da - mus

Original instrumentation

Three-part male chorus, 2 small flutes, 2 oboes, 2 clarinets, 2 trumpets, 2 horns, 3 trombones, 2 "altos" (probably English horn), 2 bassoons, serpent, timpani, bass drum *tonnerre,* cymbals, snare drum

The trombones play only in the "Judex Crederis," the most exciting moment in the composition, a Larghetto-Allegro, fiery with thundering percussion.

Documented performances

Festival of the Federation, July 14, 1790 and 1791

Source

- F-Pn, MS 1.430, autograph score, for 2 small flutes, 2 oboes, 2 clarinets, 2 trumpets, 2 horns, 2 "altos," bassoons and serpent, timpani
- D-TROb Archiv Nr. Whitwell 0318, a copy of the above
- D-TROb Archiv Nr. Whitwell 1074, modern mss score

Commentary

This is a very famous composition, because its reception by the public convinced the political authorities of the value of music in communication with the public and therefore encouraged many repetitions of this kind of outdoor ceremony, and because this success gave birth to 150 following compositions. One must also, in giving due credit to Gossec, remember that no composer in history had been given such a task, of writing for so vast an orchestra to perform before 400,000 people.

Gossec's autograph score demonstrates his initial concept to be a twelve-member wind band based on the ancient French tradition of the *Les Grands Hautbois.* By writing simple music, much of it whole-notes and half-notes, it would create, through being doubled by hundreds of wind players, the effect of a great organ.

The several sections of the Mass which the music employs are twice interrupted by almost Baroque like instrumental dances. Both dances are very interesting and therefore make their inclusion in the solemn *Te Deum* seem all the more odd. Although while Praetorius (*Syntagma Musicum* III, 1619) suggests some tradition existed for such interjections in sixteenth-century church music, one would suppose in this case it was intended to create time for some movement by the numerous priests on the constructed earth altar.

Gossec introduces an unusual ornament here, in the wind accompaniment of the chorus's "Dignare, Domine," consisting of repeated quarter-notes with a waving line over the top.

One quickly discovers that any sort of trill realization sounds wrong to the ear. There is a rarely used sign of this sort in wind instrument literature meaning tremolo and this writer has found that a tremolo created by the breath creates a truly distinct, fearful sound, which was surely intended.

W. 80, Gossec, *Domine Salvum*

Original instrumentation

Three-part male chorus, 2 small flutes, 2 oboes, 2 clarinets, 2 trumpets, 2 horns, 3 trombones, 2 "altos" (probably English horn), 2 bassoons, serpent, timpani, bass drum *tonnerre,* cymbals, snare drum

Documented performances

Most likely performed at the Festival of the Federation, July 14, 1790, although accounts do not mention it.

Source

- F-Pn, MS 1.430 (appendix)
- D-TROb Archiv Nr. Whitwell 0651, a copy of the above.

Commentary

Apparently composed in an unaccompanied version for a service at Chartres on June 9, 1790. Gossec seems to have made an instrumental version of only seventeen bars for use in the July 14, 1790 festival.

W. 81, Gossec, *Hymn for July 14*

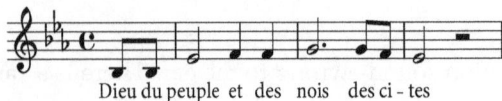

Dieu du peuple et des rois des ci - tes

Poet

M.-J. Chénier

Original instrumentation

Three-part male chorus, 2 flutes, 2 clarinets, 2 trumpets in Eb, 2 horns in Eb, 3 trombones, 2 bassoons, serpent

Documented performances

Festival of the Federation, July 14, 1791 and 1792

Source

- F-Pn, printed parts (*Magasin de musique,* Issue 17), *Hymnes et Symphonies* H2.35, Nr. 17.
- D-TROb Archiv Nr. Whitwell 0502, a copy of the above.

Commentary

This composition exists in several versions without accompaniment, and in one case with a different text. Musically the work is somewhat disappointing, lacking the inspiration of his earlier music.

The "tremolo ornament" appears again here in bar 31 of the first clarinet part.

W. 82, Gossec, *Hymne sur la translation du corps de Voltaire au Panthéon*

Ce ne sont plus des pleurs

Poet

M.-J. Chénier

Original instrumentation

Unknown

Documented performances

- The Ceremony for Voltaire, July 11, 1791
- Concert of January, 1792

Source

- F-Pn, *Musique Nationale* H2.52, a version for solo voice, 2 clarinets, 2 horns and 2 bassoons
- D-TROb Archiv Nr. Whitwell 0659, *Hymne sur la translation du corps de Voltaire au Panthéon* (Paris: *Magasin de musique*) for singer and bass.

Commentary

A work of only sixteen bars and of little interest. It seems doubtful that this was the version performed in the Voltaire ceremony, although Pierre says it was.

W. 83, Gossec, *Patriotic Chorus*

Peuple éveil le - toi, romps tes fers,

Poet

Voltaire

The original text dates from 1731, an opera by Voltaire set to music by Rameau. This original form was banned as being too profane, as its scene was Samson performing miracles at an Italian fair.

Original instrumentation

Three-part male chorus, 2 oboes, 2 clarinets, 2 trumpets in Eb, 2 horns in Eb, 3 trombones, 2 bassoons, serpent, timpani and *petites et grandes trompes antique* (*buccin* and *tuba curva*)

Documented performances

- The Ceremony for Voltaire, July 11, 1791
- The Federation, July 14, 1791

Source

- F-Pn, Bibl,. Cons. 10947 (Pierre), autograph score. A note in Gossec's hand reads, "in the absence of clarinets, the violins may transpose."
- D-TROb Archiv Nr. Whitwell 0573, a copy of the above.

Commentary

This is a good Gossec example, tuneful, heroic and full of energy and enthusiasm. Harmonically it is rather plain except for an occasional text-painting, as under "hideous slavery" one hears in the key of B-flat major a passing E-flat minor and C-flat major chord.

In D-TROb in my collection here one will find copies of two Revolutionary publications of songs by Gossec.

- Archiv Nr. Whitwell 0577 *Chant patriotique pour l'inauguration des bustes de Marat et de Lepelletier*, Song for *bassetaille* or tenor.
- Archiv Nr. Whitwell 0650 *Chanson patriotique sur le succès de nos armes*, for singer and bass.

W. 84, Gossec, *Hymn to Liberty*

Premier bien des mor-tels___ O li-ber-té___

Poet

M.-J. Chénier

Original instrumentation

Four-part chorus, small flute, 2 clarinets in C, 4 horns in F and C, 3 trombones, 2 bassoons, serpent and timpani

Documented performances

The Festival of Liberty, April 15, 1791

Source

F-Pn, mss parts, *Musique Nationale* H2.103 a-r, and also in *Musique Nationale* H2.68.

Commentary

This work was later arranged for orchestra for performance in the theaters. We find it uninspired and of little value.

W. 85, Gossec, *National Round*

L'inno cense est de re-tour et-ls triomphe á son tour

Poet

M.-J. Chénier

Original instrumentation

Four-part chorus, small flute, large flute, 2 clarinets in C, 4 horns in C and F, 3 trombones, 2 bassoons, serpent and timpani

Documented performances

- The Festival of Liberty, April 15, 1791
- Concert of November 20, 1793
- Festival of the Supreme Being, June 8, 1794
- Fifth Anniversary of the Bastile, July 14, 1794

Source

- F-Pn, mss parts, *Musique Nationale* H2, 103 a-r
- F-Pn H2.15, Nr. 8, *Collection Époques, Hymnes de la Révolution Française,* for solo voice, 2 clarinets, 2 horns and 2 bassoons

Commentary

This composition seems intended to be simple enough for the public to sing, even learn to sing on the spot, yet it is an effective work.

W. 86, Gossec, *Funeral Hymn*

Poet
Roucher

Original instrumentation
Unknown

Documented performances
- The Festival of Law, 1791
- The Funeral of Le Peletier, January 24, 1793

Source
Believed to be lost.

Commentary
This was composed in honor of Simoneau and was mentioned in the newspapers in 1791, but the actual music has not been known since that time.

W. 86bis, Gossec, *The Temple of Melpomene*

Poet
Unknown

Original instrumentation
Chorus and band

Documented performances
The Funeral of Le Peletier, January 24, 1793

Source
US-DW 573

Commentary
During the funeral of Le Peletier, the newspapers reported that as the body was being prepared for the procession to follow, a chorus of 1,000 voices sang a *Hymn to the Divinity of Nations* by Gossec, but no music under this title has survived.[100] It is possible that this was a Gossec work called *The Temple of Melpomene*, w. 86bis, for chorus and band, Melpomene being one of the ancient Greek goddesses, the goddess of Tragedy.

---

[100] This title is found only in Edmond Biré, *The Diary of a Citizen of Paris during the Terror* (London: Chatto & Windus, 1896), I, 303.

W. 87, Gossec, *Le Triomphe de la loi*

Sa-lut et re-spect á la loi!

Poet

Roucher

Original instrumentation

Three-part chorus, 2 small flutes, 2 oboes, 2 clarinets, 2 trumpets in F, 2 horns in F, 3 trombones, 2 bassoons, serpent, *buccin, tuba curva,* bass drum and cymbals

Documented performances

- The Festival of Law, 1791
- Concert of May 30, 1794

Source

- F-Pn, Bibl,. Cons. 10947 (Pierre), autograph score.
- F-Pn H2.2, 2 *Musique Nationale* (*Magasin de musique,* Issue 2, Nr. 2), printed parts, here omitting first and second trombone, *buccin* and *tuba curva*
- F-Pn, Vm 7 7026, another copy
- D-TROb Archiv Nr. Whitwell 0576, a copy of the above

Commentary

A note on the score says this work was later performed in honor of Simoneau, the mayor of d'Etampes. This is also the work which Swanzy associates with Gossec's *Symphonie militaire,* w. 70. It is a fine, exciting composition. The middle section has unexpected dynamic changes and a more florid style.

W. 88, Gossec, *Hymn to Liberty*

Vive á ja-mais, vi-ve la li-ber-té

Poet

M.-J. Chénier

Original instrumentation

Four-part chorus, 2 small flutes, 2 clarinets, 2 trumpets in Eb, 2 horns in Eb, 3 trombones, 2 bassoons, serpent and timpani

Documented performances

- The Federation, July 14, 1792
- Celebration of Victories, June 29, 1794
- Festival of the Fifth Sans-culottide, September 21, 1794

Source

- F-Pn H2.35, Nr. 8 *Hymnes et Symphonies,* (*Magasin de musique,* Issue 15)
- D-TROb Archiv Nr. Whitwell 0503, a copy of the above

Commentary

This is a weak effort by Gossec, perhaps hurriedly composed as we find material here previously used in w. 84 and w. 85. The "Gossec tremolo" ornament is found again here in the horn and trombone parts under the text, "Sing of Liberty! Sing of your honor." The effect here reminds one of Beethoven's attempt to create the sound of a large crowd cheering in his *Siegessinfonie* for band.

W. 89, Gossec, *Hymn to Liberty*

Touchant ré-veil came en-chan - teur

Poet

Varon

Original instrumentation

Four-part chorus, small flutes, 2 clarinets, 2 trumpets in Eb, 3 trombones, 2 bassoons and serpent

Documented performances

Festival of Reunion, August 10, 1793

Source

- F-Pn (*Magasin de musique*, Issue 5, Nr. 2), with additional horns and large flute, but omitting 1st and 2nd trombones. Another example under F-Pn Vm 7 7044.
- F-Pn (parts?) under H2 a-n.
- F-Pn, Bibl. Opera, Nr. 350, mss score (Pierre), now believed lost.
- D-TROb Archiv Nr. Whitwell 0506, a copy of the above.

Commentary

This work was later known as the "Hymn to Nature," which is more appropriate to the text. Here we have an inspired work of great expression by Gossec. The first movement is lyrical with dramatic and expressive use of dynamics. The second movement, Andantino, features a dialog between men and women with interesting harmonic colors, such as the use of an augmented chord under "regret." The final movement is heroic and noble; the accompaniment is independent throughout.

W. 90, Gossec, *Hymn to Nature*

Poet

Varon

Original instrumentation

Four-part chorus, small flute, 2 clarinets, 2 trumpets in Eb, 3 trombones, 2 bassoons, serpent and timpani

Documented performances

- Festival of Reunion, August 10, 1793
- Celebration of August 10th, 1794

Source

- F-Pn, *Musique Nationale*, H2.10, Nr. 2 (*Magasin de musique*, Issue 10, Nr. 2)
- F-Pn, H2, 35, Nr. 5 *Hymnes et Symphonies*
- D-TROb, Archiv Nr. Whitwell 0507, a copy of the above

Commentary

This work was later known as the "Hymn to Equality." It is very brief and has the mindless exhilaration of a fraternity song.

W. 91, Gossec, [without title]

Quel peuple im - men - se

Poet
Varon

Original instrumentation
Four-part chorus, 2 small flutes, 2 clarinets, 2 trumpets, 2 horns in Eb, 3 trombones, 2 bassoons, serpent and timpani

Documented performances
- Festival of Reunion, August 10, 1793
- Celebration of August 10th, 1793

Source
F-Pn Bibl. Opera Nr. 350 (Pierre), mss score, believed lost.

W. 92, Gossec, *Hymn to the Statue of Liberty*

Au-guste et con-sol-ante i - ma-ge Li-ber-té

Poet
Varon

Original instrumentation
Three-part male chorus, small flute, 2 trumpets, 2 horns, 2 bassoons

Documented performances
Festival of Reunion, August 10, 1793

Source
- F-Pn, Bibl. Cons., *Musique d'harmoine* paquet bis 2, mss parts (Pierre)
- D-TROb, Archiv Nr. Whitwell 0508, a copy of the above.

Commentary
It is apparent some of the parts have been lost; the original instrumentation was probably similar to w. 89 and w. 90. This is a simple, but effective work with an affectionate quality. The band only doubles the voices.

W. 93, Gossec, *Air des Marseillais*

sé-cles fa meux que l'on re - nom - me Bril-lez,

Poet
Rouget de Lisle

Original instrumentation
Three-part chorus, 2 small flutes, 2 clarinets, 2 trumpets, 2 horns, 2 bassoons, serpent and timpani

Documented performances
- Festival of Reunion, August 10, 1793
- Celebration of August 10th, 1794

Source
- F-Pn, *Musique Nationale,* H2.49, Nr. 4
- F-Pn, H2.151, 8a 8b (*Musique Natonale*), also F-Pn H2, 55
- D-TROb, Archiv Nr. Whitwell 0654, a copy of the above.
- US-DW, 37, an early anonymous for 222-12.

Commentary
This arrangement of France's most famous melody is direct, but a bit more syncopated to our ears. There is a 10 bar introduction for winds alone.

W. 94, Gossec, *Hymn to the Supreme Being*

Sour - ce de vé - re - té

Poet

M.-J. Chénier

Original instrumentation

Four-part chorus, small and large flute, 2 oboes, 2 clarinets, 2 trumpets in Eb, 2 horns in Eb, 3 trombones, 2 bassoons, serpent, *buccin, tuba curva,* bass drum, cymbals, *tambour turc.*

Documented performances

Festival of the Supreme Being

Source

- F-Pn, Bibl. Cons., 10946 (Pierre), autograph score (first and fifth movements)
- D-TROb, Archiv Nr. Whitwell 0536, a copy of the above.

Commentary

This is the version suppressed by Robespierre. There is evidence that some form of this composition was published and then all copies destroyed. The autograph score here has been altered, with the second, third and final movements removed in order to conform with the new version, W. 95.

W. 95, Gossec, *Hymn to the Supreme Being*

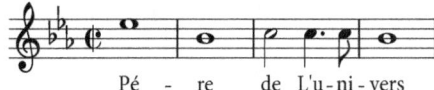

Poet

Desorgues

Original instrumentation

Four-part chorus, small and large flute, 2 oboes, 2 clarinets, 2 trumpets in Eb, 2 horns in Eb, 3 trombones, 2 bassoons, serpent, *buccin, tuba curva,* bass drum, cymbals, *tambour turc.*

Documented performances

- Festival of the Supreme Being
- Celebration of August Tenth

Source

- F-Pn, Bibl. Cons., 10946 (Pierre), autograph score
- F-Pn, *Musique Nationale,* H2.10, Nr. 2, printed parts (*Magasin de musique,* Issue 4, Nr. 2), missing parts for *buccin* and *tuba curva.* Another copy under Vm 7 7039.

Commentary

After the suppression of the Chénier text by Robespierre, Gossec decided to shorten the work to two movements. Gossec intended to create a simple work which would sound noble when sang by massed forces, as it no doubt would. There is a great deal of unison choral writing and simple homophonic writing in both movements. The "Gossec tremolo" ornament appears here in the first movement in the trombones, bassoons and serpent.

W. 96, Gossec, *Hymn to the Supreme Being*

Poet
Desorgues

Original instrumentation
Solo with choral refrain, 2 small and 2 large flutes, 2 oboes, 2 clarinets, 2 trumpets, 2 horns, 3 trombones, 2 bassoons and serpent

Documented performances
Festival of the Supreme Being

Source

- F-Pn, *Musique Nationale,* H2.4, Nr. 3 (*Magasin de musique,* Issue 4, Nr. 3). Another copy under Vm 7 7038.
- D-TROb, Archiv Nr. Whitwell 0537, a copy of the above.
- F-Pn, *Hymnes de la Révolution Française* H2.15, Nr. 22 a *Collection Époques* version of solo voice, 2 clarinets, 2 horns, 2 bassoons.

Commentary

This is the composition around which the popular legend arose of the students and faculty of the Institute of Music going out into the streets to teach a song to the public before the ceremony. The most famous characterization of this legend is a violinist, presumably Méhul, standing on a box playing this hymn before a crowd. There is no evidence to support this nice story and, indeed, the actual music makes one doubt it for the melody does not lie naturally. It is a minor effort by Gossec and not a strong composition.

W. 97, Gossec, *Hymn to Jean-Jacques Rousseau*

Toi qui d'É - mile et de So - phi - é

Poet
M.-J. Chénier

Original instrumentation
Unknown

Documented performances
- Festival of the Supreme Being, May 7, 1793
- Music in Honor of J. J. Rousseau, October 11, 1794

Source
F-Pn, *(Collection Époques) Hymnes de la Révolution Française,* printed parts for solo voice, 2 clarinets, 2 horns, 2 bassoons

Commentary
The text for this work begins with "the old people and mothers," then "representatives of the people," "young girls," etc. The work is musically uninspired, perhaps because during the three days of his composition Gossec was suffering from an inflammation of a tooth.[101]

[101] Pierre, *Les Hymnes,* 366.

W. 97bis, Gossec, *Marche funèbre à l'occasion de la mort du General Hoche*

Original instrumentation
2 flutes, 2 clarinets, 2 horns, 2 trumets, 3 trombones, 2 bassoons, serpent and bass drum

Documented performances
Unknown

Source
US-DW, Nr. 625, printed parts (Paris: Imbault)

Commentary
This funeral march is subtitled "marche lugubre," but is not the same march as w. 73.

W. 98, Gossec, *Chant funèbre sur al mort de Ferraud*

Martyr de la li - ber - té san-te

Poet

Coupigny

Original instrumentation

Solo voice with male chorus, 2 flutes, 2 oboes, 2 clarinets, 4 horns in Eb and C, 2 trumpets in Eb, 3 trombones, 2 bassoons and serpent

Documented performances

Funeral for Ferraud, June 2, 1795

Source

F-Pn, H2.100 a-p, mss parts (*Musique Nationale*)

Commentary

This is a solo work of two verses, the chorus being used only for cadences, and then becomes full hymn style for the last two verses. It is a simple composition and seems to be among Gossec's inspired works. If it is not one of his best works, one reason might be because he was given only three days to compose the music, have it printed and distributed to the members of the Convention.

> Paris, May 30, 1795
>
> I am ordered, Citizen, by the Committee of Public Instruction to send to you the attached poem on the death of our esteemed and unfortunate colleague, Feraud, who was assassinated at his post.
>
> It is the intention of the Committee that you occupy yourself wholeheartedly to setting this verse to music and having it printed in the number of 2,000 copies, in such a manner that they can be distributed to the members of the Convention and the public on the morning of the day of the funeral ceremony for representative Feraud. The copies are to be deposited with the Committee.
>
> Greetings, etc.
> Massieu

W. 99, Gossec, *Hymn to Humanity*

O mé-re des ver-tus,___ toi que la ty-ran-ne

Poet

Baour-Lormian

Original instrumentation

Four-part mixed chorus, 2 flutes, 2 clarinets, 2 horns in C, 2 trumpets in C, 3 trombones, 2 bassoons, serpent and contrabass

Documented performances

Festival of Liberty, July 27, 1795

Source

F-Pn, Bibl. Cons., *Musique Nationale,* Paquet 26, mss parts (Pierre)

Commentary

This is another composition composed on short notice, here so hurriedly the copyists were required to work all night, for two nights. As a result the work is short and uninspired.

W. 100, Gossec, *Shades of the Girondins*

Par-mi ces fu-né-bres apprets.   Ques chants.

Poet

Coupigny

Original instrumentation

Soli and four-part mixed chorus, small and large flutes, 2 oboes, solo clarinet, 2 clarinets in C, 4 horns in C and Eb, 2 trumpets in C, 3 trombones, 2 bassoons, serpent, timpani and contrabass

Documented performances

Music in Honor of the Girondins, Fall, 1793

Source

- F-Pn, Bibl. Cons., *Musique Nationale*, paquet 24, mss parts (Pierre), missing oboes, contrabass and timpani
- F-Pn, Bibl. Cons MS 10947, autograph score (Pierre)

Commentary

This is one of Gossec's best choral compositions. The form is a lengthy ABACA with good interest and variety in the subordinate sections. The work begins with a somber, dark recitative followed by a rousing, bright and optimistic chorus with good dialogs between voices and winds.

W. 101, Gossec, *Hymn to Victory*

Le peu-ple dans la nuit pro fonde_ á fait ren-trer

Poet
Coupigny

Original instrumentation
Four-part mixed chorus, small and large flutes, 2 oboes, solo clarinet, 2 clarinets in C, 2 horns in C, 2 trumpets in C, 3 trombones, 2 bassoons, *buccin* in F, *tuba curva* in C, serpent and timpani

Documented performances
Festival for the Recognition of Victories, May 29, 1796

Source

- F-Pn, Bibl. Cons., *Musique Nationale,* paquet 44, mss parts (Pierre)
- F-Pn, Bibl. Cons MS 10947, autograph score (Pierre)

Commentary
While first performed in 1796, this music had originally been part of a theater production which Coupigny and Gossec worked on together in 1794. A letter from Coupigny to Payan, a member of the Committee of Public Instruction, refers to this composition.

> The Citizen Gossec has asked me for a Hymn to Victory to be added to the act which I have done with him. I sent it to him, the music is finished, the artists are ready and the performance only awaits its examination. You have promised me you would take a look at it, it would not demand more than half an hour to examine it and in these fortunate times the composition is the order of the day.
> Coupigny

While this composition lacks the melodic and harmonic variety of Gossec's best compositions, it is nevertheless worthy of performance. It is inspired and somewhat noble.

W. 102, Gossec, *Hymn for the Celebration of Victory*

Si vous vou-lez trouver la gloi - re Cherchez

Poet
Lachabeaussière

Original instrumentation
Solo and four-part mixed chorus, 2 flutes, 2 oboes, solo clarinet, 2 clarinets in C, 2 horns in C, 2 trumpets in C, 3 trombones, 2 bassoons, serpent, timpani and *tuba curva*

Documented performances
Festival for the Recognition of Victories, May 29, 1796

Source

- F-Pn, Bibl. Cons., *Musique Nationale,* paquet 25 mss parts (Pierre), missing oboes, contrabass and timpani
- F-Pn, Bibl. Cons MS 10947, autograph score (Pierre)

Commentary
This composition appears to have been a very hurried effort.

W. 103, Horix, ?, *Marche des Français sur les bords de la Grande-Bretagne*

Original instrumentation
Flutes, 2 clarinets, 2 oboes, 2 horns, 2 trumpets, 3 trombones, 2 bassoons and percussion

Documented performance
Unknown

Source
Believed to be lost.

Commentary
Horix was a composer from Strasbourg who submitted this work to the government. It is known only by a memorandum dated March 28, 1798, signed by Cherubini and Méhul, rejecting the work on the basis of faulty harmony and instrumentation.

Hyacinthe Jadin (1769–1800)

HYACINTHE JADIN came from a very musical family which included his father and four gifted brothers. This Jadin demonstrated a gift for composition and piano by age nine and studied with Nicolas Hüllmandel, a former student of K. P. E Bach. Jadin had his first employment as a rehearsal pianist in the Feydeau Theater but before his career could really begin the Revolution broke out. Shortly after he developed tuberculosis and ended his days as the first piano professor at the Paris Conservatoire.

W. 104, Jadin, Hyacinthe, *Ouverture*

Original instrumentation
2 small clarinets, 2 horns, trumpet in F, 2 bassoons and serpent

Documented performance
Unknown

Source

- F-Pn, H2, 47, printed parts, *Magasin de musique*, Issue 13, *Musique Nationale*
- D-TROb, Archiv Nr. Whitwell 0623, a copy of the above
- F-Pn, mss parts, *Musique Nationale*, H2.132 a-m
- Modern edition: Douglas Townsend (Franco Columbo)

Commentary
The composition is very highly recommended as one of the finest instrumental works in this repertoire. It begins with a quiet lyric introduction, interrupted by dramatic unison repeated notes. The first theme is positively Mozartean.

W. 105, Jadin, H., *Hymn for January 21*

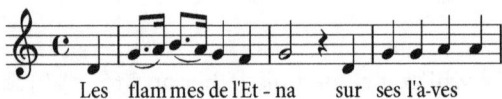

Les flam mes de l'Et - na   sur ses l'à-ves

Poet

Lebrun

Original instrumentation

Voice, 2 clarinets, 2 horns, 2 bassoons

Documented performance

Commemoration of the death of Louis XVI, 1794

Source

F-Pn, H2.15, Nr. 20, printed parts, *Collection Époques, Hymnes de la Révolution Française* H2.15, Nr. 25

Commentary

A very short composition beginning with a rousing march style, reminding one, in fact, of the Sousa, *Hands Across the Sea.* Later there is a macabre atmosphere created by repeated notes in the voice against chromatic harmony in the winds.

W. 106, Jadin, H., *Hymn to Agriculture*

Assez long temps a l'impos-tu-re L'orgueil dres-se

Poet
Lachabeaussière

Original instrumentation
Solo, chorus, small flute, 2 oboes, 2 clarinets, 2 horns, 2 trumpets in F, 2 bassoons and serpent

Documented performance
Celebration of Agriculture, June 28, 1798

Source

- F-Pn, H2., 20. *Musique Nationale,* printed parts, missing second horn and trumpets.
- F-Pn, Bibl. Cons 10949, score (Pierre)

Commentary
A work with interest and unity, but would become tedious if one sang all the verses.

Louis-Emmanuel Jadin (1768–1853)

Louis-Emmanuel Jadin came from a large family of musicians who worked for the court, hence he and his brother were born at Versailles. Like his brother Hyacinthe, Louis was famous in Paris as a pianist and accompanist and succeeded his brother as professor of piano at the Conservatory. This man found time to be a prolific composer and left among his other music some thirty-eight operas. Like Gossec he had the rare ability to be popular with the government, whether monarchy of revolutionary.

W. 107, Jadin, Louis, *Symphony*

Original instrumentation
2 small flutes, 2 clarinets, 2 horns, trumpet in F, 2 bassoons and serpent

Documented performance
Festival of the Fifth Sans-culottide, Sept. 21, 1794

Source

- F-Pn, H2.4, 1 (*Magasin de musique*), Issue 4, Nr. 1, printed parts. Also *Musique Nationale*, H2.4, 1 and Vm 7 7037.
- D-TROb, Archiv Nr. Whitwell 0613, a copy of the above
- F-Pn, H2.132 a-m, *Musique Nationale*, mss parts
- Swanzy, 177-189, mss score
- Modern edition, William Schaefer (Shawnee) and (Friedrich Hoffmeisster-Verlag)

Commentary
This is light in character but one of Jadin's better efforts.

W. 108, Jadin, L., *Ouverture*

Original instrumentation

2 small flutes, 2 large flutes, 2 oboes, 2 clarinets, 2 horns in C, 2 trumpets in C, 2 bassoons, trombone, serpent and timpani

Documented performance

Unknown

Source

- F-Pn, H2., 6,1. *Musique Nationale* (*Magasin de musique,* Issue 6, Nr. 1) printed parts. Another copy under Vm. 7 7048.
- D-TROb, Archiv Nr. Whitwell 0618, a copy of the above.
- Swanzy, 220-238, mss score
- Modern edition, US-DW 1705 (Suppan)

Commentary

Here is a very interesting work, quite above average and worthy of performance. It begins with a dark, dramatic introduction, followed by an Allegro with bright lyrical themes. The development section is very interesting harmonically.

W. 109, Jadin, L., *Marche*

Original instrumentation
2 small flutes, 2 clarinets, 2 horns, 2 trumpets in F, 2 bassoons and serpent

Documented performance
Unknown

Source

- F-Pn, H2., 7, 3. *Musique Nationale* (*Magasin de musique,* Issue 7, Nr. 3), printed parts
- D-TROb, Archiv Nr. Whitwell 0636, a copy of the above.

Commentary

An excellent example of the short march form. It is vigorous, full of drive and difficult in the cadences with their thirty-second-note figures.

W. 110, Jadin, L., *Pas de manoeuvre*

Original instrumentation
2 small flutes, 2 clarinets, 2 horns, 2 trumpets in F, 2 bassoons and serpent

Documented performance
Unknown

Source

- F-Pn, H2., 7, 4. *Musique Nationale* (*Magasin de musique,* Issue 7, Nr. 4), printed parts
- D-TROb, Archiv Nr. Whitwell 0646, a copy of the above.

Commentary

Other than the Trio which resembles a Bach harmonic exercise, this march has no particular character.

W. 111, Jadin, L., *Hymn of the Freed Slaves*

Au jour plus pur qui té - clai - re ou vre les yeux, ô mon fils!

Poet

Coupigny

Original instrumentation

2 small flutes, 2 clarinets, 2 horns, 2 trumpets in F, 2 bassoons and serpent

Documented performance

Spring, 1794

Source

- F-Pn, H2., 3, 6. *Musique Nationale* (*Magasin de musique,* Issue 3, Nr. 6), printed parts. Another copy under Vm 7.7036
- D-TROb, Archiv Nr. Whitwell 0652, a copy of the above.

Commentary

A work composed at the request of the Convention following their action earlier in the year of abolishing slavery.

W. 112, Jadin, L., *Hymn to J.-J. Rousseau*

En-fin sur les bords de la Sei - ne

Poet

Désorgues

Original instrumentation

Chorus, 2 flutes, 2 clarinets, 2 horns, 2 trumpets in F, 2 bassoons and serpent

Documented performance

Ceremony in Honor of J. J. Rousseau, October 11, 1794

Source

- F-Pn, *Musique Nationale*, H2.18, mss score, perhaps autograph
- F-Pn, H2., 108, a-m, mss parts
- D-TROb, Archiv Nr. Whitwell 0584, a copy of the above.

Commentary

An undistinguished work, yet better than the one on the same subject by Gossec. The Trio carries the note, "Based on three notes of J. J. Rousseau."

Rodolphe Kreutzer (1766–1831)

Rodolphe Kreutzer was born to a German father who worked for the French Court. He was a prolific composer whose works include 19 violin concerti and 40 operas. He was best known, however, as a violinist and as one of the original violin professors of the Paris Conservatory. His name will never be forgotten as he was the dedicatee of Beethoven's Violin Sonata, Nr. 9, Op. 47 (1803). Kreutzer himself never performed Beethoven's Sonata, declaring it unplayable and incomprehensible. Nevertheless, when Beethoven got into a quarrel with the original dedicatee, George Bridgetower, he revised the dedication in favor of Kreutzer.

W. 113, Kreutzer, *Ouverture*, "Journée de Marathon"

Original instrumentation

2 small flutes, 2 clarinets in C, 2 horns, trumpet in C, 2 bassoons, serpent, bass trombone and timpani

Documented performance

Ceremony in Honor of J. J. Rousseau, October 11, 1794

Source

- F-Pn, H2, 9, 1 *Musique Nationale* (*Magasin de musique,* Issue 9, Nr. 1), printed parts
- D-TROb, Archiv Nr. Whitwell 0656, a copy of the above.
- Dudley, II, 75-90, mss score

Commentary

Nice ideas, poorly developed.

Honoré Langlé (1741–1807)

REMEMBERED PRIMARILY AS A THEORIST, Langlé was devoted to composing operas and performing as a keyboard artist in concerts of chamber music in Paris. Among his keyboard students was the queen, Marie Antoinette. When the Royal School of Singing was created in 1784 he became a teacher of singing, but when the Conservatory was founded he became its librarian.

W. 114, Langlé, *Hymn to the Eternal*

Poet
Lebrun

Original instrumentation
Voice, 2 clarinets, 2 horns and 2 bassoons

Documented performance
Unknown

Source
F-Pn, H2, 15, Nr. 24 (*Collection Époques*)

Commentary
This work is known only from the *Collection Époques* of 1799–1800. The composition has a curious rapidly moving bass line throughout most of the work.

Xavier Lefevre (1763–1829)

LEFEVRE WAS A SWISS BORN CLARINETIST whose career was made in Paris. First a member of the French Guard band in 1778 at age fifteen, then with the National Guard band when it was formed at the time of the revolution. He was very active as a clarinet player at the Opera and as a teacher at the Paris Conservatory.

W. 115, Lefevre, *Ouverture*

Original instrumentation
Small flute, 2 clarinets, 2 horns, 2 bassoons, serpent, *buccin, tuba curva* and string bass

Documented performance
Unknown

Source
F-Pn Bibl. Cons. *Musique d'harmonie,* paquet 22 (Pierre)

Commentary
The labeling of the original parts indicate an incomplete set when cited by Pierre. In the reorganized National Library I was unable to locate this Overture.

(W. 116-127), Lefevre, *(Collection)*

Original instrumentation
2 flutes, 2 clarinets, 2 horns, trumpet, 2 bassoons, serpent, cymbals, bass drum

Documented performance
Unknown

Source
F-Pn, Vm 7.7100 (Paris: Imbault), printed parts

Commentary
Pierre erred in his measure count, therefore I have given the correct length in bars after the titles. Only w. 121, w. 124 and w. 127 are worthy of consideration for performance.

W. 116, *Marche,* (24 bars)

W. 117, *Marche,* (18 bars)

W. 118, *Marche,* (25 bars)

W. 119, *Marche,* (52 bars)

W. 120, *Marche,* (22 bars)

W. 121, *Marche,* **(41 bars)**

W. 122, *Pas redoublé,* **(16 bars)**

W. 123, *Pas redoublé,* **(24 bars)**

W. 124, *Pas redoublé,* **(24 bars)**

W. 125, *Pas redoublé,* **(24 bars)**

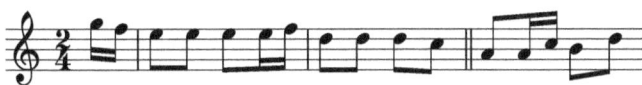

W. 126, *Pas redoublé,* **(24 bars)**

W. 127, *Pas redoublé*

W. 128, Lefevre, *Marche militaire*

Original instrumentation

2 flutes, 2 clarinets in C, 2 horns, trumpet, trombone, 2 bassoons, serpent and timpani

Documented performance

- Ceremony in Honor of J. J. Rousseau
- Concert of November 7, 1794

Source

- F-Pn, H2, 9, 1 *Musique Nationale* (*Magasin de musique,* Issue 2, Nr. 3), printed parts. Another copy is found under Vm 7.7027.
- D-TROb, Archiv Nr. Whitwell 0627, a copy of the above.

Commentary

This is an excellent march, one of the most musical in this repertoire. To my ears it sounds more in the old Imperial style rather than in the newer more sedate Classical style of most of these marches.

W. 129, Lefevre, *Pas de manoeuvre*

Original instrumentation
Two small flutes, 2 clarinets, trumpet in F, 2 horns, trombone, 2 bassoons and serpent

Documented performance
Unknown

Source

- F-Pn, H2, 2, 4 *Musique Nationale* (*Magasin de musique,* Issue 2, Nr. 4), printed parts. Another copy is found under Vm 7.7028.
- D-TROb, Archiv Nr. Whitwell 0640, a copy of the above.
- F-Pn, Bibl. Cons. 10947 (Pierre), mss score in the key of G major.

Commentary
One of the best examples of the Pas de manoeuvre form.

W. 130, Lefevre, *Hymn*

Poet
Unknown

Original instrumentation
Chorus, flutes, oboes, clarinets, horns, bassoons, trumpets, trombones, serpent and timpani

Documented performance
Anniversary of the Death of Louis XVI, January 21, 1795

Source
Believed to be lost.

Commentary
A copyist's invoice indicated parts for 35 singers and 42 instrumentalists.

W. 131, Lefevre, *Hymn to Agriculture*

Mé-re commu-n des hu mains,   Je te sa-lue

Poet

Coupigny

Original instrumentation

Four-part mixed chorus, 2 flutes, 2 clarinets, 2 horns, 2 bassoons, 2 trumpets in F, 3 trombones and serpent

Documented performance

Festival of Agriculture, June 28, 1796

Source

- F-Pn, Bibl. Cons. 10949 (Pierre), mss. score
- F-Pn, Bibl. Cons. *Musique nationale*, paquet 30 (Pierre), mss score and parts

Commentary

Lefevre appears to have taken his assignment seriously, including a nicely constructed opening. The result, however, is a bit simplistic and dull.

Jean François Lesueur (1760–1837)

LESUEUR BEGAN HIS MUSIC EDUCATION and early employment in a number of cathedrals, eventually becoming director of music at Notre Dame in Paris. He was appointed to the newly formed Institute of Music and when it became the Paris Conservatory he was made an inspector. His better known colleagues, Méhul and Gossec, relegated him to teaching only elementary harmony. This, plus the rejection of his opera, *Ossian,* in place of one by Catel, caused Lesueur to publish a violent pamphlet, *Projet d'un plan général de l'instruction musicale en France,* attacking the Conservatory and resulting in his dismissal. Now he was reduced to poverty until Paisiello recommended him to Napoleon as head of the music of the Tuileries. Back in favor, he was now able to rejoin the faculty of the Conservatory where twelve of his students won the famous *Prix de Rome,* including Berlioz and Gounod.

W. 132, Lesueur, *Hymn of the Triumphs of the French Republic*

Original instrumentation
Chorus, oboes, clarinets, horns, bassoons, cymbal and bass drum

Documented performance
Concert of November 7, 1794

Source
F-Pn, Bibl. Cons. *Mus. pour inst. à vent,* paquet 39 (Pierre)

Commentary
Pierre believed this and the following work were somehow related to the major composition W. 133.

W. 133, Lesueur, *Hymn of the Triumphs of the French Republic*

Quand___ des mon - ta - gnes de Py - ré - ne

Poet

La Harpe

Original instrumentation

Four-part chorus, 2 flutes, 2 oboes, 2 clarinets in C, 2 trumpets, 2 horns, 2 bassoons, 3 trombones, serpent and timpani

Documented performance

Concert of November 7, 1794

Source

- F-Pn, *Magasin de musique,* Issue 9, Nr. 2 in *Musique nationale* H2l. 9, 2.
- D-TROb, Archiv Nr. Whitwell 0559, a copy of the above.

Commentary

This is not a bad composition, with lots of variety. Curiously the published edition has the choral parts in C minor and the band part in D minor. Was he anticipating that the singers would sing *that* sharp?

W. 134, Lesueur, *Patriotic Scene*

C'est peu d'a-voir ob-te-nu la vic-tor-re Braves franéais

Poet

Dercy

Original instrumentation

Male chorus, small and large flutes, 2 oboes, 2 clarinets in C, 2 trumpets, 4 horns in C and Eb, 2 bassoons *"de choeur,"* 2 bassoons *"d'accompagnement,"* 3 trombones, serpent, *tuba curva*, string bass and timpani

Documented performance

Concert of November 7, 1794

Source

F-Pn, Bibl. Cons., *Musique nationale,* paquet 34 (Pierre), mss parts, but missing all the band parts except first clarinet

Commentary

This is a very long composition, like a scene from an opera. The choral parts vary from dull to moments of real beauty. It is impossible to say more, given the lost band parts, but Pierre quotes, without attribution, this contemporary review:

> The chorus by Citizen Lesueur makes a fine effect by the arrangement of the parts, their total effect, which permits hearing all the words and the slightest detail of the band.

I should mention that in my Trossingen, Archiv-Nr. Whitwell 0518, there is a copy of a Lesueur score for mixed chorus and orchestra, *Chant national pour l'anniversaire du 21 Janvier, choeur Nr. 23,* to words by Lebrun.

W. 135, Lesueur, *Hymn for July 27*

Le - vons nous, un tribun per - fi - de De - son

Poet
Desorgues

Original instrumentation
Voice, 2 clarinets, 2 horns, bassoons

Documented performance
Unknown

Source
F-Pn, H2, 15, Nr. 30, *Hymnes de la Révolution Française (Collection Époques)*, printed parts

Commentary
This is a simple song in a popular style, probably with little interest for the modern audience.

W. 136, Lesueur, *Hymn for the Inauguration of a Temple of Liberty*

O li-ber-té li-ber-té sainte dé-es-se d'un peup-ple

Poet
François de Neufchâteau

Original instrumentation
Voice, 2 clarinets, 2 horns, bassoons

Documented performance
Unknown

Source
F-Pn, H2, 15, Nr. 17, *Hymnes de la Révolution Française (Collection Époques)*, printed parts

Commentary
This is apparently the original version and is a nice example of the repertoire for single voice. A short work with an engaging melody, easy and affectionately conceived.

W. 137, Lesueur, *Chant dithyrambique*

Ré-veil-le-toi   ly - re d'Or-phé - e

Poet
Lebrun

Original instrumentation
Unknown

Documented performance
Festival of Liberty and the Arts, July 27, 1798

Source
F-Pn, H2, 15, Nr. 39, *Hymnes de la Révolution Française (Collection Époques),* printed parts for voice, 2 clarinets, 2 horns and 2 bassoons

Commentary
This is not an interesting composition; a similar version exists for full symphonic orchestra.

W. 138, Lesueur, *Hymn for the Festival of Argiculture*

Al-lons   a - mis de la - bour-ra - ge, Poussez

Poet
François de Neufchâteau

Original instrumentation
Unknown

Documented performance
Festival of Agriculture, June 28, 1798

Source
F-Pn, H2, 15, Livre second, Nr. 7, *Hymnes de la Révolution Française (Collection Époques),* printed parts for voice, 2 clarinets, 2 horns and 2 bassoons

Commentary
The original poem was sung to the *Marseillaise* melody. A very singable popular song. The accompaniment sounds rural.

W. 139, Lesueur, *Hymn for Old Age*

Ce jour__ est le jour__ des vain-quers

Poet

d'Arnajult

Original instrumentation

Voice, 2 clarinets, 2 horns and 2 bassoons

Documented performance

Festival of Old Age, 1799

Source

- F-Pn, H2, 15, Livre second, Nr. 10, *Hymnes de la Révolution Française (Collection Époques),* printed parts
- F-Pn, MS 4713 mss (Autograph?) score

Commentary

This is an excellent solo example. A nice melodic style with a middle section which is more quiet and contemplative.

Johann Paul Schwartzendorf, known as Martini il Tedesco, (1741–1816)

SCHWARTZENDORF SHOWED EARLY PROMISE in his native Neuburg, Germany, and began music studies at age ten in Friburg. Returning home on one occasion he discovered a new stepmother and decided immediately to leave home. But where to? He climbed to the roof of his father's barn and threw a feather into the air, determined to go in whatever direction the feather blew. The feather floated west, and so the young man ended up in Paris where he adopted a family name, Martini. On the day he arrived in Paris he found it was the closing day of a competition to create a new march for the Swiss Guards Band. Martini wrote the march which won the contest on that very evening. He went on to work for several important courts and churches. In 1800 he became a professor of composition at the Paris Conservatory, but was forced out due to political manoeuvring by Méhul and Catel. After the restoration he became superintendent of court music.

One of his popular ballads, "Plaisir d'amour" was used in 1961 by Elvis Presley as the basis for one of his pop standards, "Can't Help Falling in Love."

W. 140, Martini, *Hymn to the Republic*

Que now voix, nos ly-res al tié-res

Poet
M.-J. Chénier

Original instrumentation
Four-part chorus, small and large flutes, 2 oboes, 2 clarinets, 2 trumpets, 2 horns, bass trombone, 2 bassoons, serpent, contrabass, bass drum and cymbals

Documented performance
Federation, 1798

Source

- F-Pn, Bibl. Cons., *Magasin de musique,* Issue 22, paquet 35 (Pierre), printed parts
- F-Pn, H2, 15, Livre second, Nr. 1, *Hymnes de la Révolution Française (Collection Époques),* printed parts for a version for solo voice, 2 clarinets, 2 horns and 2 bassoons

Commentary
This has a lengthy instrumental introduction, which, like the entire composition suffers from too much repetition, too many running diatonic scales and little melodic interest.

W. 141, Martini, *Triumphal Hymn for the Festival of September 22*

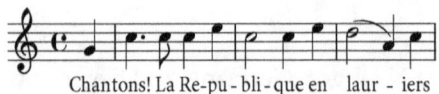
Chantons! La Re-pu-bli-que en laur-iers

Poet

Leclerc

Original instrumentation

Four-part mixed chorus, small and large flutes, 2 clarinets, 2 oboes, 2 horns, 2 bassoons, trombone, serpent, string bass, bass drum and cymbals

Documented performance

Federation, 1798

Source

F-Pn, Bibl. Cons., *Musique nationale*, paquet 43 (Pierre), printed parts

Commentary

A lengthy work of some 200 measures which mixes mythology and Republican heroes. An introduction of more than 40 bars is unusual, but in general this is a dull work.

Étienne Méhul (1763–1817)

MÉHUL BECAME ONE OF THE MOST HIGHLY RESPECTED COMPOSERS in Paris and was one of the first Frenchmen to receive the *Légion d'honneur.* He began as the son of a poor cook and wine merchant and his first musical studies were with a blind organist. One can understand, therefore, that he was largely self taught and indeed he once said that between 1787 and 1790 he composed four operas just for practice. Certainly it was only after 1790 that his reputation as a stage composer began to grow. He became one of the five inspectors of the new Paris Conservatory and had a personal relationship with Napoleon. Unfortunately he died young, in 1817, from tuberculosis.

W. 142, Méhul, *Ouverture*

Original instrumentation
2 small flutes, 2 clarinets, 2 trumpets, 2 horns, 2 bassoons, bass trombone, serpent and timpani

Documented performance
- Concert of May 30, 1794
- The Festival of the Worship of Reason, November 10, 1793
- Celebration of August Tenth, 1794
- Concert of November 7, 1794

Poet
- F-Pn, *Magasin de musique,* Issue 3, Nr. 1 in *Musique nationale* H2.3, 1. Another copy can be found under Vm 7.7031.
- D-TROb, Archiv Nr. Whitwell 0617, a copy of the above.
- F-Pn, D.7.855, a mss score contemporary with Méhul
- F-Pn, H2. 135 a-q, mss parts
- Modern edition (New York: Southern Music Corp.)

Commentary
One of the best compositions of the Revolutionary repertoire. A slow and dramatic beginning is followed by themes of almost Mozartean grace and elegance. A new theme in the development section is haunting and dramatic.

W. 143, Méhul, *Le Chant du départ*

La victoire en chan-tant Nous ou - vre la barriere

Poet

M.-J. Chénier

Original instrumentation

Solo with choral refrain, 2 clarinets, 2 trumpets, 2 bassoons, serpent and timpani

Documented performance

- Music for the Celebration of Victories, June 29, 1794
- Fifth Anniversary of the Bastille, July 14, 1794
- Festival of the Fifth Sans-culottide, September 21, 1794
- Celebration of August Tenth, 1794
- Anniversary of the Fall of the Bastille, July 14, 1797

Source

- F-Pn, *Magasin de musique,* Issue 6, Nr. 2 in *Musique nationale* H2.6, 2. Another copy can be found under Vm 7.7049.
- D-TROb, Archiv Nr. Whitwell 0597, a copy of the above.
- F-Pn, H2.15, Nr. 16. *(Collection Époques), Hymnes de la Révolution Française,* for solo voice, 2 clarinets, 2 horns and 2 bassoons
- Modern edition (New York: Southern Music Corp.)

Commentary

During its time this was one of the most respected compositions of the Revolutionary repertoire, but to our ears it is rather simple and uninteresting. Nevertheless, as I have said, this work had great impact in its time. A local newspaper, *Duchosal,* specifically mentioned this composition after hearing it in the Festival of the Celebration of August Tenth.

> When one hears the *Chant du départ,* one thinks one hears Plato with these words: "Tremble enemies of France." The rage was painted in all the faces, and the spectators appeared all agitated.[102]

[102] Quoted by Pierre in *Les Hymnes,* 346.

W. 144, Méhul, *Le Chant des victoires*

Fuy-ant ses ill-es conster-né - es   l'l - bé - re orgueilleux

Poet

M.-J. Chénier

Original instrumentation

Chorus, flutes, clarinets, horns, trumpets, trombones, bassoons, serpents, string bass, *buccin*, cymbal, bass drum

Documented performance

- Celebration of August Tenth, 1794
- Festival of the Fifth Sans-culottide, September 21, 1794

Source

F-Pn, H2.15, Nr. 28. *(Collection Époques)*, *Hymnes de la Révolution Française,* H2.15, Nr. 28, printed parts for voice, 2 clarinets, 2 horns and 2 bassoons

Commentary

The original full band version of this work has been lost.

W. 145, Méhul, *Funeral Hymn for Feraud*

Un deuil ré-li-ge-eux couvre au loin la Pa - tri - e

Poet

Baour-Lormian

Original instrumentation

Voice, 2 small clarinets, 2 trumpets, 2 horns, 3 trombones, 2 bassoons, and serpent

Documented performance

Funeral Ceremony in Honor of Feraud, June 2, 1795

Source

- F-Pn, Bibl. Cons., *Musique nationale*, paquet 38 (Pierre), mss parts, missing second horn. Another copy can be found under Foly.688.
- F-Pn, H2.15, Nr. 33. *(Collection Époques)*, *Hymnes de la Révolution Française*, printed parts for solo voice, 2 clarinets, 2 horns and 2 bassoons

Commentary

This composition is original and inspired with variety and interest. It is not a great example, but it is a worthy one.

W. 146, Méhul, *Hymn for July 27*

Sa-lut neuf thermi-dor___ jour de la dé-il-vran --ce

Poet

M.-J. Chénier

Original instrumentation

Voice, 2 clarinets, 2 horns and 2 bassoons

Documented performance

Festival of Liberty, July 27, 1793

Source

F-Pn, H2.15, Livre second, Nr. 8. *(Collection Époques), Hymnes de la Révolution Française*

Commentary

This is a later version, with an entirely new melody, on a text originally used by Méhul in a song for voice and basse. This composition is in a popular, singable style, but not too interesting musically.

W. 147, Méhul, *Hymn of the Twenty-Two*

Républi-cains dont le gé - ni - e Vainqu-it

Poet

M.-J. Chénier

Original instrumentation

Solo, four-part mixed chorus, 2 small flues, 2 clarinets, 2 trumpets, 2 horns, 3 trombones, *buccin* in F, 2 bassoons, serpent, string bass, timpani, bass drum and cymbals

Documented performance

Music in Honor of the Girondins, Fall, 1793

Source

- F-Pn, Bibl. Conc., *Musique nationale,* paquet 37 (Pierre) mss parts
- F-Pn, H2.15, Nr. 35. *(Collection Époques), Hymnes de la Révolution Française,* printed parts for solo voice, 2 clarinets, 2 horns and 2 bassoons

Commentary

Begins with a rather dull introduction followed by an outstanding choral allegro, featuring much dynamic unison writing. The second verse is for the "women and children" of the twenty-two and the third verse is for the "ghosts" of the twenty-two.

W. 148, Méhul, *Le Chant du retour*

Contemplez nos lauriers ci - vi - ques

Poet
M.-J. Chénier

Original instrumentation
Four-part mixed chorus and band, instrumentation unknown

Documented performance
Ceremony of Campo-Formio, December 10, 1797

Source
F-Pn, H2.15, Nr. 40. *(Collection Époques), Hymnes de la Révolution Française,* for solo voice, 2 clarinets, 2 horns and 2 bassoons

Commentary
All of the original wind parts are lost; only the choral parts survive. This is to be regretted as the extant *Collection Époques* version reveals a rousing and worthy composition of substantial length.

W. 149, Méhul, *Hymn for the Festival of Marriage*

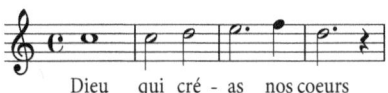
Dieu qui cré - as nos coeurs

Poet
Ducis

Original instrumentation
Voice, 2 clarinets, 2 horns and 2 bassoons

Documented performance
Festival of Marriage, 1799

Source
F-Pn, H2.15, Livre second, Nr. 5 *(Collection Époques), Hymnes de la Révolution Française*

Commentary
This is a simple and dignified composition which would make an interesting program number for modern audiences.

Étienne Ozi (1754–1813)

OZI WAS BORN IN NISMES where he first studied in a military ensemble. Moving to Paris in 1777 he made numerous solo appearances as a bassoonist with the concerts of the Concert Spirituel. While on the faculty of the Free School of Music and later the Paris Conservatory he produced a great mass of educational materials for his instrument, some of which are still used today.

W. 150, Ozi, *Pas de manoeuvre*

Original instrumentation

2 small flutes, 2 oboes, 2 clarinets in Eb, trumpet in F, 2 horns, 2 bassoons and serpent

Documented performance

Unknown

Source

- F-Pn, *Magasin de musique,* Issue 3, Nr. 4 in *Musique nationale* H2 3, 4. Another copy can be found under Vm 7 7034.
- D-TROb, Archiv Nr. Whitwell 0641, a copy of the above.

Commentary

Subtitled, "Rondeau," a form similar to the early march form, may be the best of the *Pas de manoeuvre* repertoire. For himself to play it has a running bass line in sixteenth-notes.

W. 151, Ozi, *Pas de manoeuvre*

Original instrumentation

2 small flutes, 2 oboes, 2 clarinets in Eb, trumpets in F, 2 horns, 2 bassoons, 3 trombones, and serpent

Documented performance

Unknown

Source

- F-Pn, *Magasin de musique,* Issue 12, Nr. 4 in *Musique nationale* H2.12.4.
- D-TROb, Archiv Nr. Whitwell 0648, a copy of the above.

Commentary

Subtitled "Rondeau" a happy work and nice example of the form in the meter of 6/8.

Niccolo Piccinni (1728–1800)

PICCINNI WAS A VERY PROLIFIC COMPOSER OF OPERA, of which he composed six in a single year, 1761. His opera buffa, *La Cecchina,* was very successful, with a two-year run in Rome. At the time he was more popular even than Pergolesi, with whom together they formed a new kind of opera culminating in Mozart. He was invited to Paris by Marie Antoinette where he also enjoyed wide success. With the beginning of the French Revolution Piccinni returned to Naples, where the marriage of his daughter to a French democrat brought him disgrace and he was placed under house arrest for four years. For the next nine years he lived a life of destitution. Upon his return to Paris in 1798 his works again received great applause and to help him Napoleon gave him a commission to compose a march and arranged for him to teach at the Conservatoire.

W. 152, Piccinni, *Hymn for the Festival of Marriage*

Dieu d'hymen re-cois now hom-mages

Poet
Ginguené

Original instrumentation
Two voices, 2 oboes, 2 clarinets, 2 horns and 2 bassoons

Documented performance
Festival of Marriage, 1799

Source
F-Pn, H2.15, Livre second, Nr. 11 *(Collection Époques); Hymnes de la Révolution Française.*

Commentary
This work has some charm, but all in all is not very interesting. There is an informative letter from the poet to Sarrette which confirms the eternal nature of bureaucracy.

To Citizen Sarrette, Commissaire for the organization of the Conservatory of Music, Conservatory, rue Bergère

Paris, March 1, 1799

I was counting, Citizen, on giving a course this morning at the conservatory. The beautiful weather invited me there, but affairs have retained me. Piccinni who came with you to my house the other day, said to me, after your departure, that he had already begun to concern himself with my hymn; but that as he had not yet received the official invitation, he believed it necessary to wait for it before proceeding any further. It appears, in effect, Citizen, that the invitation for the music must be given to him in the same form the invitation for the poetry was given to me. I have known first of all from you that Piccinni would be in charge of this composition. I then spoke to the Minister who confirmed this decision. I sent my verses to Piccinni asking him to work with them, saying he would receive from the Minister or you, Citizen, an official invitation. Please be so kind as not to delay any longer this small formality without which it is only natural the composer does not wish to proceed. The first chorus of the hymn is done and it is very charming. I am very impatient to see the rest. One says that the printing of the collection advances; there is no time to lose. I recommend this object to your diligence and honesty, Citizen.

Ginguené

Ignaz Pleyel (1757–1831)

PLEYEL WAS BORN THE SON OF A SCHOOL TEACHER and was the 24th of 38 children. A local noble felt sorry for the family and, at the birth of the 24th child, offered to educate him. This led to Pleyel's great advantage in studying with both Vanhal and Haydn. His first extensive employment was in the Strasbourg cathedral, 1783–1795, and at this time he also wrote a number of works for Harmoniemusik. After the French Revolution abolished church performances Pleyel went to London where he made a fortune. In Paris, as a foreign born person he was nearly imprisoned by the Committee of Public Safety but was saved due to some pro-revolution compositions he had written in Strasbourg. After the revolution Pleyel became an unusually successful businessman, founding a publishing company and as a manufacturer of pianos.

W. 153, Pleyel, *Hymn to Liberty*

Poet
Rouget de Lisle

Original instrumentation
Two voices, 2 oboes, 2 clarinets, 2 horns and 2 bassoons

Documented performance
Festival to celebrate the new Constitution, Strasbourg, 1791

Source
F-Pn, H2.15, Nr. 9 *(Collection Époques); Hymnes de la Révolution Française.*

Commentary

The original version of this work is lost, but an account by the poet, Rouget de Lisle, in his *Essais en vers et en prose, 1796,* of the performance in Strasbourg documents a much larger instrumentation.

> This hymn dates from the beginning of the Revolution, it was performed at Strasbourg for the celebration of the publication of the first constitutional act ... it was performed in the open air at the place d'Armes, performed by a colossal orchestra

conducted by Pleyel himself. The musicians first played a strophe, then it was repeated by the immense population, which filled the square to its limits and to which was attached the military bands of all the numerous regiments attached to the garrison ...

Translated into German, it passed over the Rhine River and was sung by the inhabitants of Brisgaw. Often I, on the free side, heard being sung on the other shore this song consecrated to French liberty.[103]

[103] Quoted in Pierre, *Les Hymnes,* 218.

In 1979 I was the guest conductor at a chamber music festival in Breitneich, Austria, near the village where Pleyel was born. Following the final paragraph above, my host, a Viennese aristocrat, organized a Harmoniemusik performance playing some of Pleyel's own compositions in that village on Pleyel's birthday. The idea was, as above, to let the sound of the free music drift across the river into what was then Communist controlled Eastern Germany.

Henri Joseph Riegel (1741–1799)

RIGEL WAS A GERMAN COMPOSER LIVING IN FRANCE, who had studied in Italy with the famous Niccolò Jommelli. He moved to Paris in 1767 where he had much success as a keyboard performer, but little recognition as a composer in spite of a number of compositions, including fourteen operas.

W. 154, Rigel, *Hymn to Liberty*

Poet
Baour-Lormian

Original instrumentation
Four-part mixed chorus, small flute, 2 clarinets, 2 trumpets, 2 horns, 2 bassoons, serpent, string bass and timpani

Documented performance
Celebration of August Tenth, 1795

Source

- F-Pn, Bibl. Cons., 10949 (Pierre) mss score
- F-Pn, bibl. Cons., *Musique nationale,* paquet 39 (Pierre), mss parts

Commentary
This a brief, engaging work which is effective and not difficult.

Claude Rouget de Lisle (1760–1836)

ROUGET DE LISLE FIRST ENLISTED IN THE ARMY as an engineer, attaining the rank of captain. As a royalist, he refused to take the oath to the new constitution and lost his job, was thrown into prison in 1793 and narrowly escaped the guillotine. As an amateur poet he had the rare fate of composing the most popular national tune in French history, the *La Marseillaise*.

W. 155, Rouget de Lisle, *Roland à Roncevaux*

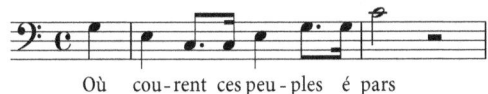

Où cou-rent ces peu-ples é pars

Poet
Rouget de Lisle

Original instrumentation
Unknown

Documented performance
Celebration of the Girondins, October, 1795

Source

- F-Pn, Bibl. Cons., *Musique nationale,* paquet 40 (Pierre), mss parts called *Hymn of War*

- F-Pn, Bibl. Cons., *Musique d'harmonie,* paquet 30, b (Pierre), mss parts for 2 clarinets, 2 trumpets, 2 horns and bassoon

- F-Pn, H2.15, Nr. 11 *(Collection Époques), Hymnes de la Révolution Française,* printed parts for solo voice, 2 clarinets, 2 horns and 2 bassoons

Commentary

This is a fine war song, heroic and noble. The composer later recalled,

One tries to recapture here the famous ballad of Rolland which was the war song of our ancestors, and of which no one today has any vestige ... Like those of today, the French were fighting for their lives against the Moors, who after conquering Spain, were attempting to submit Europe to despotism. Only the times and customs change.

An extant note written by Sarrette to the editors of the *Collection Époques* recommends bringing the work into closer relationship to the revolution, changing the title to *Song of War* and suggesting some textual changes ("Do you see these proud mecreans" to "Do you see these bloody soldiers?")

Pierre wrote that he could not believe that this work was originally composed for band, but admits it was the only form that appeared in official ceremonies. We believe the musical evidence, such as the fanfare quality of the cadences, argue for the band composition.

Étienne Solère (1753–1817)

Solère was a French composer, clarinetist and music educator. He was playing in a military band at age fourteen and in Paris studied with Michel Yost. As a soloist he toured Italy, Spain and Russia and became principal clarinetist in the king's orchestra in Paris. He founded a music school, the *Conservatoire national supérieur de musique* in Paris. One early source maintains he wrote seventy-five suites for Harmoniemusik.

W. 156, Solère, *Ouverture*

Original instrumentation
2 small flutes, 2 clarinets, trumpet in F, 2 horns, 2 bassoons and serpent

Documented performance
Unknown

Source

- F-Pn, *Magasin de musique,* Issue 11, Nr. 1; *Musique Nationale* H2.11, 1
- D-TROb, Archiv Nr. Whitwell 0622, a copy of the above.
- Dudley, II, 111-121, mss score

Commentary
This is a boring and tedious work.

Jean Pierre Solié (1755–1812)

SOLIÉ WAS A CELLIST AND SINGER, for whom Méhul composed some roles especially for him. He began composition rather late, yet composed thirty-three operas, mostly one-act stage works.

W. 157, Solère, *Pas de manoeuvre*

Original instrumentation
2 small flutes, 2 clarinets, trumpet in F, 2 horns, 2 bassoons and serpent

Documented performance
Unknown

Source

- F-Pn, *Magasin de musique,* Issue 10, Nr. 4; *Musique Nationale* H2.10, 4
- D-TROb, Archiv Nr. Whitwell 0647, a copy of the above

Commentary
This work has little of interest.

Johann Christoph Vogel (1756–1788)

VOGEL WAS A GERMAN COMPOSER who first moved to Paris in 1776, joining the court ensemble of Duke of Montmorency as a second horn player. He was active in attempting to compose opera, but his ideal was Gluck and so the public heard them as being old fashioned. His final opera, *Démophon,* was left unfinished due to his early death at age thirty-two.

W. 158, Vogel, *Ouverture to Démophon*

Original instrumentation
Unknown

Documented performance

- Funeral Service for the Victims of the Nancy Affair, September 20, 1790
- Music for the Fifth Anniversary of the Bastille

Source

- F-Pn, Bibl. Cons., *Musique d'harmonie,* paquet 30a (Pierre), mss parts
- F-Pn, Bibl. Cons., *Musique d'harmonie,* paquet 11 (Pierre), an arrangement by F. G. Fuchs (Paris: Sieber) for 4 clarinets, 2 horns, 2 bassoons, trumpet and serpent
- F-Pn, Vm 7 4287, a published late nineteenth-century piano arrangement by Léon Chic

Commentary

I was not able to find in the National Library either of the two sources mentioned by Pierre. Based on the piano version it had a fairly interesting introduction but the rest was undistinguished. Nevertheless, an early French dictionary reported that the work was performed in 1791 on the Champ de Mars by 1,200 wind instruments with "unparalleled success."

Part III

Band Music for Festivals under the Restoration of the Bourbons

THE GREAT FESTIVALS OF THE FRENCH REVOLUTION discussed above were fuelled in great part by the turbulence of constantly changing political objectives. This period, 1790–1799, of struggle for political power ended relatively abruptly with the appearance of a new dictator, Napoleon. Civic participation in government was now replaced by the public's participation in the Napoleonic Wars.

By the time Napoleon was removed from power he had left behind the loss of an entire generation of young Frenchmen, among whom some have estimated 2,000 musicians. In considering this cost of territorial glory, the French people now began to think perhaps a resumption of the long French history of kings was not such a bad idea. The allies who had defeated Napoleon now restored the throne to the brothers of King Louis XVI who had been beheaded during the revolution. These following two kings, Louis XVIII (1814–1824) and Charles X (1825–1830), returned France to a much more conservative government.

The climate of civic participation which had been so evident during the Revolution now found a role in local, rather than national, activities. In Music this meant a very dynamic new period of civic orchestra, band and choral societies being formed throughout the country. Now there were local festivals celebrating poets, people like Gutenberg and the inauguration of civic buildings, bridges, etc.

On rare occasions the national government still organized an event for the purpose of focusing the attention of the public on something above the local level. One such festival in Paris was in honor of those killed in the July Revolution of 1830.[104] For this festival the government commissioned Hector Berlioz to compose a musical work which, as in the festivals of old, would be the centerpiece of the ceremonies. The result was a Symphony for band and the complete title makes it sound like something which might have been composed in 1790–1799, *Grande Symphonie Funèbre et Triomphale composee pour la Translation des restes des victims de Juillet et l'inauguration de la colonne de la Bastille.*

[104] The decline in the popularity of Charles X, together with continued economic hardships of the general public, resulted in a new king, Louis-Philippe in 1830. There were some killed among the public protesters of the government at this time and they were remembered later as the Victims of the July 1830 Revolution.

National moments such as this reawakened in some the memories of the great festivals of 1790–1799. This brief period, in turn, produced three of the greatest compositions in the repertoire of the wind band. The following discussion is to introduce these three masterpieces to those who may not know them. After 200 years these compositions are still in print and may be ordered through www.maximesmusic.com.

The Anton Reicha Symphony for Band

Adagio-Allegro
Adagio, Theme and Variations
Marche funebre, Maestoso un poco adagio
Poco Presto

THIS SYMPHONY IS ONE OF THE GREAT MONUMENTS of the repertoire for the wind band. To fully understand the unique nature of this score one must first recall the late eighteenth century tradition of the great public festivals in Paris during which a large wind band, composed by bringing together numerous smaller bands, played a central role. And so it followed that Anton Reicha, a gifted composer then living in Paris,[105] anticipated that another one of these great festivals might be organized.[106] It seems clear that his purpose, in 1815, was to create in advance a composition suitable for such a great outdoor performance. In the same spirit as Beethoven, who first dedicated his *Third Symphony* to Napoleon and then changed his mind and scratched out the dedication on the autograph score, Reicha apparently realized that a work dedicated to Napoleon would have a very brief performance life and so he outlined a much broader purpose. While the title on the autograph score reads, "Symphony without strings" (*Harmonie complete ou Symphonie sans insts. à cordes*), in his handwritten preface Reicha identifies his purpose:

> This work is composed to commemorate: 1st, the memory of great exploits; 2nd, the death of heroes and great men; 3rd, to celebrate any important future event.

[105] Anton Reicha (1770–1836), after moving to Paris became a highly respected professor at the Paris Conservatoire and among his students were Liszt, Berlioz and Gounod.

[106] Indeed such a festival did occur in 1815, but it was a Church festival held in Notre Dame. The musical result was a magnificent *Requiem for Louis XVI and Marie Antoinette* for chorus and large wind band by Charles N. Bochsa and a similar *Requiem in C minor* by Cherubini, which as yet has not been found.

It was to make his Symphony practical, no matter how vast the open air space might be, that Reicha created a form based on the principle of the Baroque *Concerto grosso*. This explains the curious appearance of the autograph score, where one sees in normal musical notation a symphony for one wind band, but in the margins, expressed in a special numeric code, his directions where additional wind bands could enter and exit in the manner of the old seventeenth-century *concertato* style. He makes this clear in a note in the score where he writes, "*Cette Symphonie est Concertante.*" In terms of the *concerto grosso* tradition it seems clear that Reicha considered the music in the score (music for one band) to be the *concertino*, the principal ensemble, while the other two bands represented by his marginal code were the *ripieno*, or the additional ensembles which join the *concertino* from time to time. This is what he refers to in his preface when he says the extra parts are for use in music performed in honor of France *(Les parties detaches de la musique en l'honneur de la Nation française.)*

The autograph score of this *Symphony for Band* has one more note in the hand of Reicha which is of considerable interest and curiosity. But first it is necessary to make two brief quotations from his autobiography.

> I have never been interested in writing for the popular demand. To enlighten the public has been my aim; not to amuse it ... Many of my works have never been heard because of my aversion to seeking performances ... I counted the time spent in such efforts as lost, and preferred to remain at my desk ...
> It is impossible to discuss my complete works here. More than a hundred have been published; about sixty are still in manuscript. Among the latter will be found my finest efforts.

It is known that he kept some of his "finest efforts" in a trunk. All this is important as background for one additional note in his autograph score. He says the score of this symphony for band is found in a collection of scores (*Catalogue Nr. 1 Partition*) together with the rest of the volumes of band music in code (*et il y a dans le meme volumes des Sceruirs d'harmonie*). Taken with the above quotations, one is tempted to think that perhaps Reicha, who had a local reputation for his interest in mathematics, had further works for band abbreviated in some kind of code similar to the one used in this Symphony. I believe whatever he was referring to remains a complete mystery.

In his autograph preface Reicha also makes interesting comments about acoustics and says the performance must be assigned to a good conductor, all of which are very rare comments for 1815. He also adds,

> It is imperative to use the exact number of instruments mentioned in the score, otherwise the work would not sound as effectively. These instruments are: 3 piccolos, 6 oboes, 6 clarinets, 6 horns, 6 bassoons, 6 trumpets, 3 double-basses, 6 army drums and 4 small field-guns.

He amends this to give approval for contrabassoons as an alternative to the string basses. The instrumentation he gives above is for the principal band with two additional *ripieno* bands. The instrumentation of the primary band alone, the only parts given actual musical notation, is piccolo, pairs of oboes, clarinets, horns, bassoons, and trumpets, plus bass [string bass or contrabassoon].

THE QUESTION REMAINS, how does one perform this magnificent music today? If one decides to perform the original version, as given above, then one encounters several difficult problems. First, one has in hand the only score in 600 years of original band repertoire which requires *nine* separate bassoon parts! One significant challenge is finding three contrabassoons. When I performed the original version in 1974 I used one my university owned and the one owned by the LA Philharmonic, but the search for a third instrument in good condition was surprisingly difficult. Also, in my 1974 performance, I found that a considerable distance between these three bands was necessary in order for the listener to understand that they were in fact separate ensembles. That is, since all three bands play the same notes in unison, the ear tends not to sort things out into three divisions. As a result, for a good effect from the audience perspective a very large stage is required, something rarely found in most universities or civic institutions.

In my desire to make this beautiful music available to future students, I next tried to score the work for one modern band, but having the "extra" bands identified through dissimilar instrumentation. This, to my ear, had an even worse result, for it sounded like a composition for band with an extra jazz band and brass band.

Finally, in recognition of the fact that the composer heard in his mind and wrote down actual music for one band, the extra bands written in code, again, being given only doubling parts in unison, and, as the reader has seen above, described first a Symphony without strings and separately a work which could be used "in honor of France," I began to think of this symphony as one for only one band. This for me was the key, for I realized it was still possible to make an edition for modern band of just the principal part which could result in a performance that still sounded like a work written in 1815, still sounded like Reicha and captured throughout his beautiful music.

FINALLY, BOUND TOGETHER with the three original movements of the Symphony is a work for the same instrumentation, but minus the flutes, called a *funèbre marche*. It is not clear whether Reicha expected this work to be a movement in the symphony, for he comments "It was principally for the army that I composed this marche funèbre, which may be performed alone." It is a beautiful and noble work and I accept it as part of the symphony because it has the same instrumentation, even the four cannons. The missing flutes probably reflects the fact that the army did not use the flute, but rather the fife. Finally because he allows that "it can be performed alone" an alternative is assumed, and that must be the symphony with which it is bound.

The Nicholas Charles Bochsa Requiem for Louis XVI and Marie Antoinette

After Napoleon was first defeated by a coalition of European powers in 1814, the coalition restored the throne of France to Louis XVIII on April 6, 1814. Louis XVIII returned to Paris on April 24, 1814, and the subsequent celebration of the Bourbon Restoration was the occasion for a Motet, by Bochsa, "Composed for the celebration of the Apothéose of Louis XVI and the Happy Return of the Bourbons."

After "The Hundred Days," during which Napoleon attempted to regain control, another, much larger celebration was held on January 15, 1815, centered on the reburial of the remains of Louis XVI and Marie Antoinette. It was for this celebration that Bochsa and Cherubini composed Requiems in honor of Louis XVI.

The Requiem for Louis XVI and Marie Antoinette

Louis XVI had been beheaded on January 21, 1793, as a victim of the French Revolution. But France had always been a country with a father-figure at the head of society and after the period during which Napoleon was responsible for the death of an entire generation of French young men during his European Wars, the public began to look back to the harmless old king, Louis XVI. This turn in sentiment resulted in the reburial of Louis and his wife in a more suitable location. And so on the anniversary of Louis' beheading, on

January 21, 1815, a great ceremony was held in Paris which featured two government commissioned Requiems, one by Cherubini and one by Bochsa.

The importance of this occasion can be seen in the fact that on the very same day in Vienna an identical ceremony to commemorate Louis XVI was held in St. Stefan's Cathedral, organized by Talleyrand as an official event during the Congress of Vienna. The music on this occasion was a *Requiem* by Sigismund Neukomm, with Salieri conducting. Neukomm, whose birthplace was Salzburg,[107] wrote a number of large-scale compositions for band which are unknown today.

Charles Nicholas Bochsa (1789–1856) was the son of Charles Bochsa, an oboist and conductor of a French regimental band who later moved to Paris to become a publisher. The son, Charles Nicholas Bochsa, was a prodigy performing a piano concerto in public at age seven, a flute concerto of his own composition at age eleven and the following year composing a ballet. As a student at the Paris Conservatoire he studied with Catel and Méhul and while still in the Conservatoire he joined with Erard, the piano manufacturer, to invent the double action harp. For this instrument Bochsa produced a vast number of studies which are still used today.

In 1813 Napoleon appointed Bochsa as the official harpist to his court and in this same year Bochsa began to compose the first of seven works for the Opéra-Comique. The *le Journal des débats* of 16 September 1815 looked back over these stage works and found that Bochsa's music had "warmth, dramatic truth and, as they say, youth."[108]

On becoming an extremely well-known musician in Paris, Bochsa, perhaps under the pressure of having to associate with very successful and wealthy persons, began to create various kinds of letters of credit, forging the signatures of a large number of people and institutions for the purpose of obtaining money from their private accounts. One contemporary found that Bochsa had stolen 760,000 francs. To escape a court order for his arrest, branding and years of hard labor, Bochsa fled to London.

---

[107] Just around the corner from a house I maintained there for two years.

[108] Quoted in Michel Faul, *Nicolas-Charles Bochsa* (Le Vallier: Editions Delatour France, 2003), 17. Faul quotes many reviews from Bochsa's English residence.

In London, Bochsa, by nature a showman, introduced himself by organizing eye-catching concerts such as one at Covent Garden for thirteen harps, an oratorio, *Le Déluge universal*, for chorus, fourteen harps and double orchestra and composed his only opera in English, *A Tale of Other Times*. His most successful idea was to found, in 1823, the Royal Academy of Music, a school patterned after the Paris Conservatoire. Soon, however, there were rumors of "freedom taken with the code of conduct" and Bochsa was forced out of the direction of the school in 1826.

It was at this time that Bochsa began his association with Anna Rivière, a very talented soprano who became the wife of Sir Henry Bishop, known locally as "the English Mozart" and already famous as the composer of the song, "Home, Sweet Home."[109] They met and began to become close during her appearances with the King's Theatre and the Italian Opera House, where Bochsa had become Musical Director. She was rapidly becoming famous and Bochsa, to take advantage of this, eloped with her and began to accompany her on extensive recital tours throughout Europe, including the Scandinavian countries, Russia and Italy, where Bochsa was appointed Director of the Regio Teatro San Carlo.

In 1847, the couple sailed for America and performed in New York, Boston, Washington, Baltimore, Richmond, Charleston, Savannah and New Orleans. While passing through America, a review of one of their recitals appeared in the *American Review* for 1846, the reviewer found the singing of Anna Bishop to be rather cold and not from the heart. Of Bochsa the review was more complimentary.

[109] From his opera, *Clari* (1829).

> Bochsa is another instrumental wonder. The harp in his hands is full of splendid effects; it is capable of infinite variety in power and quality of tone, full of delicacy and of lyric fire. His execution is wonderful, and the variety of his touch still more so. His hands wander all over the strings and produce sounding arpeggios, rapid sparkling passages above, and harmonics as pure and silvery as we may imagine to come from the golden-wired harps of the cherubims. Few, who never heard such playing, can be aware of the scope of the

instrument in solos, or indeed of its peculiar effects in the hands of such a master, as an accompaniment to the voice.

In 1849 Bochsa and Anna, whom he introduced as his pupil, made a nine-month tour of Mexico and in a journal[110] she kept we learn some personal characteristics of Bochsa. Here we read that Bochsa, at age sixty, was rather well-known for the "rotundity of his form,"[111] near-sighted, an imposing figure who spoke with "startling emphasis."[112] Reviews[113] of his performance in Mexico City indicate that even at this advanced age Bochsa remained a great harpist.

[110] *Travels of Anna Bishop in Mexico, 1949*, published without an author's name by Charles Deal in Philadelphia in 1852.
[111] Ibid., 14, 42.
[112] Ibid., 212, 147, 126.
[113] Ibid., 104ff.

> He is, incontestably, the greatest harpist ever listened to.
> *Trait d'Union*
>
> Clear as the tones of a nightingale in his touch, he completely overrules every difficulty of this undocile instrument, and, by the power of his genius, draws from it such torrents of harmony as overwhelm the audience with delight and wonder.
> *Siglo XIX*
>
> Bochsa's harp solo is dwelt upon, as a composition of the most exquisite brilliancy and a performance of incredible power and beauty.
> *La Moda*

While in Mexico City, Bochsa actually composed, in three days time, an *Operatta buffo, El Ensayo*, to be sung in Spanish. In its review of this performance, the paper *El Monitor* reminded its readers that Bochsa was known not only as the "Paganini of the Harp," but "as a composer of great skill and fecundity."

> Our limit of space will not permit us to analyze, as carefully as we would, this inspiration of one of the most celebrated composers of the age. It is rich in ideas, piquant and original, and the instrumentation is performed with that thorough knowledge of the orchestra, possessed by Bochsa to so high a degree of mastery.

They then returned to North America, giving many recitals, but now Bochsa's health was beginning to fail. The newspaper *Daily Alta California* posted a notice on 8 July, 1855:

> We understand the old composer and conductor is in a precarious state of health and is afraid he will never leave California. A great musical light goes out.

Nevertheless, by December 1855 they were sailing again, now for Sydney, Australia. Within a month of their arrival, Bochsa died. A long cortège of local musicians formed a procession to his burial place, performing the slow movement of Beethoven's *Third Symphony* and marches taken from the works of Handel. His broken-hearted companion commissioned an elaborate tomb, which shows her lying at the base of a tree with a harp lying against it, in the Camperdown Cemetery in Sydney, and reading,

> Sacred
> To the memory of
> Nicholas Charles Bochsa, Esq.
> Who died 6th January 1856
> This monument is erected in sincere
> Devotedness by his faithful friend and pupil
> Anna Bishop
>
> ———
>
> Mourn him—mourn his harp-strings broken
> Never more shall float such music
> None could sweep the lyre like him!

Half a world away and six months later, an Irish newspaper carried a brief obituary.

> Mr. Elia's Record for this week announces the death, in Australia, of Signor Bochsa, a man who, had he possessed more conduct and less charlatanry, might have left a permanent name in the annals of music, and not merely in Europe an ephemeral reputation, which, for better or worse, had died out long before he himself had died. Signor Bochsa was an original and brilliant harpist, allowing for a certain flashy vulgarity of taste, which seemed to cleave to all the man's doings. Some of his music for his instrument, both solo and concerted, has fancy and wel intented (or adroitly borrowed) ideas.

The Cork Examiner, 6 June, 1856

After Bochsa's death. Anna continued her life as a traveling artist, with concerts in Asia (where she was wrecked on Wake Island and stranded for three weeks), India, back to Australia and then to New York where she died in 1884.

The Hector Berlioz Symphony for Band

Grande Symphonie Funèbre et Triomphale

Marche Funèbre
Oraison Funèbre
Apothéose

Manuscript score

Partial autograph score F-Pn [MS. 1164]. This extant score is the final of several earlier versions destroyed by the composer.

First edition

Paris: Schlesinger, October, 1843

Modern edition

David Whitwell, www.maximesmusic.com

I would really have no hesitation in placing this composition ahead of the other works of Berlioz: it is noble and elevated from the first note to the last …; a sublime patriotic enthusiasm, which rises from the strains of lamentation to the highest peaks of apotheosis, preserves this work from any exaltation of an unseemly kind.

I grant further to Berlioz the merit of having used, in a style that is thoroughly noble, the music of a military wind-band, which was all that was available to him on this occasion. I must therefore withdraw what I was saying earlier about the future fate of the works of Berlioz, at least as far as this *Symphonie de Juillet* is concerned … I must express with joy my conviction that this symphony will endure and exalt the courage of people so long as a nation with the name of France endures.

Richard Wagner, *Le Ménstreal*, Paris, 5 May 1841

First Version of the Score

Symphonie Militaire [Lost]

We are unlikely to find the original version of this great monument of the wind band's repertoire as it has long been lost. Commissioned by the Minister of the Interior in Paris, it was intended to be the central musical feature of a ceremony on 28 July 1840 commemorating the reburial of the remains of some of the victims of the tenth anniversary of the "July Revolution."

The first to be heard were the initial two movements, played by a military band marching through Paris. This music must have been quite different from the Symphony we know today. Certainly the second movement which we know today as a very free recitative, would be unsuitable for performing while marching—not to even consider Berlioz' claim that he conducted it walking backward! And, of course, the second movement had a completely different name.

But the first movement of the version we know must have been simplified for street use. This is reflected not only in some simplified fragments which have survived,[114] but also in Berlioz' recollection in his autobiography, "I thought that the simplest plan would be best for such a work."[115]

We have important insights regarding the original first movement provided by two important early music historians[116] who actually saw this first score before it was lost. The most significant observation is found in Pohl where the keys of the horns are given as E-flat, G and D. The keys of these natural horns would correspond with the final two movements as we know them, but not the first movement. The inescapable conclusion is that the original [street version] of the first movement may have been in another key.

The possibility of an entirely different first movement [street version] perhaps is related to the fact that the version we know today has a tam-tam part in the first movement, but not in the following movements. As the use of a tam-tam was frequently found in the processional band music

[114] These may be seen in David Whitwell, "Concerning the Lost Versions of the Berlioz Symphony for Band," *Journal of Band Research* (Vol. XI, Nr. 2), Spring, 1975, 5.

[115] *Memoirs of Hector Berlioz* (New York: Dover, 1966), 232.

[116] J. G. Prod'homme, *Hector Berlioz* (Paris, 1927), 1238 and Louise Pohl, *Hector Berlioz' Leben und Werke* (Leipzig, 1900), 140.

of the French Revolution, this may be an indication that the organizers had in mind following the tradition of those famous outdoor ceremonies of the earlier period.

If we lack the physical details of the original version of this Symphony, we are in no doubt what Berlioz had in mind regarding his purpose.

> I wished to begin with to recall the conflicts of the famous Three Days amidst the mourning strains of a bleak but awe-inspiring march, to be played in the procession; to follow this with a kind of funeral oration or farewell address to the illustrious dead, while their bodies were lowered into the cenotaph, and to conclude with a hymn of praise at the moment when, the tomb being sealed, all eyes were fixed on the high column on which Liberty with wings outspread seemed soaring toward Heaven like the souls of those who had given their lives for her.
>
> ...
>
> I was held up for quite a long time over the fanfare which I wanted to bring gradually up from the depths of the orchestra to the high note on which the song of triumph bursts in. I wrote version after version. None of them satisfied me. ... I imagined a trumpet-call of archangels, simple but sublime, boundless, glittering, an immense radiance swelling and resounding, proclaiming to earth and heaven the opening of the Empyrean gates.[117]

[117] *Memoirs*, 253ff.

Beginning in the following month, August 1840, the administration of the Salle Vivienne allowed Berlioz to organize concerts by way of introducing the new Symphony to the public in an indoor symphonic setting. It should be noted that in these first indoor concerts the first movement was omitted, suggesting that Berlioz was at work in creating a new version. Here, as would be forever the case when he conducted, the audience was particularly struck by the final movement, the *Apothéose*.

> The Apothéose was interrupted five times by applause. At the return of the triumphal theme, all of the audience was on its feet moving about, screaming—it was superb.[118]

[118] Letter to his Sister, Adele, Paris, November 2, 1840.

The initial reactions of the public are striking.

> Your music is beautiful—very beautiful and it is very successful. All of the connoisseurs have admired your generous and lofty style—it is frank, new and beautiful.
> Edmond Cave, Office of the Minister of the Interior.

> I do not like either the man or his manners, but justice forces me to admit that ... there is a summing up which has a great impact far superior to anything he has written so far.
> Adolphe Adam, composer

> I must tell you that never before has music made me feel such emotions. It was beautiful, grand and beyond anything I could have imagined ... Bless you a thousand times! I would like to tell you a little about what I feel now and the admiration and respect that I have for you, but words fail me! My heart is too full, too full.
> Letter to Berlioz from August Luchet, Nogent-sur-Maine, August 12, 1840.

Second Version of the Score

Symphonie Funèbre [Lost]

On 1 February 1842 Berlioz conducted the third of these Salle Vivienne concerts. Here we see in the program that he has given it a new title, *Symphonie Funèbre,* although in a letter to his sister Nanci, 5 February, he was still calling it his *Symphonie Militaire.* A program two weeks later gives for the first time the full title as it is usually given today, *Grand Symphonie Funèbre et Triomphale.*

Now for the first time strings have been added and in future performances Berlioz often referred to the work as a *Symphony for Two Orchestras.* While the Symphony is often printed today with strings at the bottom, doubling the band, there existed now a new manuscript score ["despite the expense of a double orchestra and the new copy"], which has been lost.

Again Berlioz experiences an enthusiastic public response to the last movement.

> [If you could be] among the shouts, the cries, the entire feeling that excited the Apothéose of my Symphonie Militaire that I have just rescored for two orchestras. The moment the second

orchestra played part of the audience stood up in a great agitation and the two hundred musicians could no longer be heard, such was the force of the unsuppressed shouts.[119]

[119] Letter to his Sister, Nanci, Paris, February 5, 1842.

It was a performance of this version which the then very famous Spontini heard and wrote, "I write still being under the impression of your vibrant music."[120]

[120] *Memoirs*, 253ff.

Third Version of the Score

Symphonie Funèbre et Triomphale [Lost]

In a letter to his sister, Nanci, July 5, 1842, he calls this score a "new version" and here we not only find the addition of a chorus, but now for the first time the second movement carries the name we know, *Oraison Funèbre*. This new version of the Symphony with chorus was first performed, but without strings, on September 26, 1842, in the Concert Hall of the Royal Brussels Military Band.

The addition of a text to sing, beginning with this version, certainly contributed to the difficulties of performance. Berlioz found a text by Antoni Deschamps (1800–1869), which he decided to lay over his existing music. Always a difficult practice [usually music is added to text], in this case there are moments when the result is almost unsingable, even for French singers.

This "new version" Berlioz must have decided had reached its final form for it is clear in his correspondence that he believed the work would soon be published. As had long been the custom, a composer would dedicate a new publication to a member of the royal family, in return for which he expected a handsome donation. Thus we find a manuscript score cover in Berlioz' hand dedicating this Symphony to Ferdinand Philippe, the current Duke of Orléans, a lover of the arts, and talented artist himself. The Duke had no sooner accepted the dedication by Berlioz when, in a fall from his carriage, he died on 13 July 1842 at the age of thirty-two.

Although Berlioz was disappointed by his bad luck in this regard, this autograph cover page plays an important role in dating the gradual development of this score toward its final form. This cover reappears attached to the final version of the Symphony which is housed today in the National Library in Paris. Seen today this page, the sole survivor of this version of the score, is very worn, badly torn and soiled from use and has been attached to the new and never used final extant version made by his copyist, Rocquemont. I regard this single page, removed from a previous score, to be the remaining fragment of the version of the score which Berlioz now began to carry around and perform in foreign cities.

One of these trips to present his compositions by being their guest-conductor was to Brussels where he conducted the band of the *Société de la Grande-Harmonie.* In a letter arranging for the various details of the concert, Berlioz now provides the most extensive title of the Symphony to date, *Grande Symphonie Funèbre et Triomphale composee pour la Translation des restes des victims de Juillet et l'inaugration de la colonne de la Bastille.* For us this marriage of title and purpose, like Anton Reicha's earlier band symphony written for Paris in 1815, *Commemoration Symphony, Musique pour célébrer la mémoire des grands hommes,* has an echo of the great festivals of the French Revolution.

On the stage and pit of the Paris Opera house later this year, on 7 November 1842, the Symphony in its complete version, for band, orchestra and chorus, was heard for the first time.

Extant Manuscript Version of the Score

F-Pn [MS. 1164]

And now we come to the partial autograph score which resides in Paris today, which has attached to it the cover page in the hand of Berlioz from an earlier version. This 1843 score is a "presentation score" and begins with a few pages in the hand of Berlioz and then continues in the hand of his copyist. After this "presentation score" was completed, the earlier version both men were copying from was destroyed.

But while this partial autograph score has every appearance intending to be the final version, the sudden reappearance of the hand writing of Berlioz on page 71 and on pages 106 and 107 indicates that he was still composing as this "final" copyist score was in progress. What was he doing?

One of these brand new passages includes the extraordinary abrupt shift (it can hardly be called a modulation) from B-flat to A major. This passage contains a reference to the "Dresden Amen," which we believe is a tribute to his friendly association with Mendelssohn during a German tour and the latter's *Reformation Symphony* which uses this cadence extensively. It is a most heart-lifting and thrilling conclusion for the symphony.[121] The other passage in the hand of Berlioz in this "final" score is a strengthened final cadence. Here, while waiting for Berlioz to supply his latest changes, we can see the bored copyist filling the margins of the score paper with doodles.[122]

The publication of this "final" score by Schlesinger in the Fall of 1843 includes even more changes, though minor. And finally, the composer's famous treatise on instrumentation was published in December 1843 and it contains a quotation from this symphony. The manuscript for the treatise[123] contains autograph corrections on nearly every page and the subsequent published form has still further changes!

[121] Mendelssohn and Berlioz did not get along well when they first met in Rome as young men. Subsequent letters before Berlioz' arrival in Leipzig on his tour make it clear that both men were nervous about this reunion. However, they got along in splendid fashion, Berlioz mentioning that Mendelssohn treated him "like a brother" during the month they were together in Leipzig.

[122] A copy of these doodles can be seen in David Whitwell, "Concerning the Lost Versions . . . ."

[123] Now in the Bibliotheque de Grenoble.

About the Author

DR. DAVID WHITWELL is a graduate ("with distinction") of the University of Michigan and the Catholic University of America, Washington DC (PhD, Musicology, Distinguished Alumni Award, 2000) and has studied conducting with Eugene Ormandy and at the Akademie für Musik, Vienna. Prior to coming to Northridge, Dr. Whitwell participated in concerts throughout the United States and Asia as Associate First Horn in the USAF Band and Orchestra in Washington DC, and in recitals throughout South America in cooperation with the United States State Department.

At the California State University, Northridge, which is in Los Angeles, Dr. Whitwell developed the CSUN Wind Ensemble into an ensemble of international reputation, with international tours to Europe in 1981 and 1989 and to Japan in 1984. The CSUN Wind Ensemble has made professional studio recordings for BBC (London), the Köln Westdeutscher Rundfunk (Germany), NOS National Radio (The Netherlands), Zürich Radio (Switzerland), the Television Broadcasting System (Japan) as well as for the United States State Department for broadcast on its "Voice of America" program. The CSUN Wind Ensemble's recording with the Mirecourt Trio in 1982 was named the "Record of the Year" by *The Village Voice*. Composers who have guest conducted Whitwell's ensembles include Aaron Copland, Ernest Krenek, Alan Hovhaness, Morton Gould, Karel Husa, Frank Erickson and Vaclav Nelhybel.

Dr. Whitwell has been a guest professor in 100 different universities and conservatories throughout the United States and in 23 foreign countries (most recently in China, in an elite school housed in the Forbidden City). Guest conducting experiences have included the Philadelphia Orchestra, Seattle Symphony Orchestra, the Czech Radio Orchestras of Brno and Bratislava, The National Youth Orchestra of Israel, as well as resident wind ensembles in Russia, Israel, Austria, Switzerland, Germany, England, Wales, The Netherlands, Portugal, Peru, Korea, Japan, Taiwan, Canada and the United States.

He is a past president of the College Band Directors National Association, a member of the Prasidium of the International Society for the Promotion of Band Music, and was a member of the founding board of directors of the World Association for Symphonic Bands and Ensembles (WASBE). In 1964 he was made an honorary life member of Kappa Kappa Psi, a national professional music fraternity. In September, 2001, he was a delegate to the UNESCO Conference on Global Music in Tokyo. He has been knighted by sovereign organizations in France, Portugal and Scotland and has been awarded the gold medal of Kerkrade, The Netherlands, and the silver medal of Wangen, Germany, the highest honor given wind conductors in the United States, the medal of the Academy of Wind and Percussion Arts (National Band Association) and the highest honor given wind conductors in Austria, the gold medal of the Austrian Band Association. He is a member of the Hall of Fame of the California Music Educators Association.

Dr. Whitwell's publications include more than 127 articles on wind literature including publications in *Music and Letters* (London), the *London Musical Times*, the *Mozart-Jahrbuch* (Salzburg), and 50 books, among which is his 13-volume *History and Literature of the Wind Band and Wind Ensemble* and an 8-volume series on *Aesthetics in Music*. In addition to numerous modern editions of early wind band music his original compositions include five symphonies.

David Whitwell was named as one of six men who have determined the course of American bands during the second half of the twentieth century, in the definitive history, *The Twentieth Century American Wind Band* (Meredith Music). A doctoral dissertation by German Gonzales (2007, Arizona State University) is dedicated to the life and conducting career of David Whitwell through the year 1977. David Whitwell is one of nine men described by Paula A. Crider in *The Conductor's Legacy* (Chicago: GIA, 2010) as "the legendary conductors" of the twentieth century.

> "I can't imagine the 2nd half of the 20th century—without David Whitwell and what he has given to all of the rest of us."
> Frederick Fennell (1993)

About the Editor

CRAIG DABELSTEIN began studying the piano at age seven and took up the saxophone at age twelve. Mr Dabelstein has Bachelor of Arts (Music) and Bachelor of Music degrees from the Queensland Conservatorium of Music and a Graduate Diploma of Learning and Teaching and a Graduate Certificate in Editing and Publishing from the University of Southern Queensland. He has held the principal saxophone chairs in the Australian Wind Orchestra and has been an augmenting member of the Queensland Philharmonic and Symphony Orchestras. He was a member of the Queensland Saxophone Quartet and has previously been a saxophone teacher at the Queensland Conservatorium of Music. He is a regular conductor of the Queensland Wind Orchestra and has been a research associate for the *Teaching Music Through Performance in Band* series of books. He is the editor of more than forty books by Dr. David Whitwell including *A Concise History of the Wind Band, Foundations of Music Education, Music Education of the Future, The Sousa Oral History Project, Wagner on Bands, Berlioz on Bands, The Art of Musical Conducting, Aesthetics of Music* (8 volumes) and *The History and Literature of the Wind Band and Wind Ensemble* (13 volumes). He currently teaches saxophone and clarinet, and conducts bands at St Joseph's College, Gregory Terrace.

Books by David Whitwell

- The Sousa Oral History Project
- The Art of Musical Conducting
- The Longy Club: 1900–1917
- La Téléphonie and the Universal Musical Language
- Extraordinary Women
- A Concise History of the Wind Band
- Essays on the Modern Wind Band
- Essays on Performance Practice
- A New History of Wind Music
- The College and University Band
- The Early Symphonies of Mozart
- Music of the French Revolution
- Stories from the Podium

On Composers

- Wagner on Bands
- Berlioz on Bands
- Chopin: A Self-Portrait
- Liszt: A Self-Portrait
- Schumann: A Self-Portrait in His Own Words
- Mendelssohn: A Self-Portrait in His Own Words

On Education

- Philosophic Foundations of Education
- Foundations of Music Education
- Music Education of the Future

Aesthetics of Music

- Aesthetics of Music in Ancient Civilizations
- Aesthetics of Music in the Middle Ages
- Aesthetics of Music in the Early Renaissance
- Aesthetics of Music in Sixteenth-Century Italy, France and Spain
- Aesthetics of Music in Sixteenth-Century Germany, the Low Countries and England
- Aesthetics of Baroque Music in Italy, Spain, the German-Speaking Countries and the Low Countries
- Aesthetics of Baroque Music in France
- Aesthetics of Baroque Music in England

The History and Literature of the Wind Band and Wind Ensemble Series

- Volume 1 The Wind Band and Wind Ensemble Before 1500
- Volume 2 The Renaissance Wind Band and Wind Ensemble
- Volume 3 The Baroque Wind Band and Wind Ensemble
- Volume 4 The Wind Band and Wind Ensemble of the Classical Period (1750–1800)
- Volume 5 The Nineteenth-Century Wind Band and Wind Ensemble
- Volume 6 A Catalog of Multi-Part Repertoire for Wind Instruments or for Undesignated Instrumentation before 1600
- Volume 7 Baroque Wind Band and Wind Ensemble Repertoire
- Volume 8 Classical Period Wind Band and Wind Ensemble Repertoire
- Volume 9 Nineteenth-Century Wind Band and Wind Ensemble Repertoire
- Volume 10 A Supplementary Catalog of Wind Band and Wind Ensemble Repertoire
- Volume 11 A Catalog of Wind Repertoire before the Twentieth Century for One to Five Players
- Volume 12 A Second Supplementary Catalog of Early Wind Band and Wind Ensemble Repertoire
- Volume 13 Name Index, Volumes 1–12, The History and Literature of the Wind Band and Wind Ensemble

Ancient Voices

- Ancient Views on Music and Religion
- Ancient Views on the Natural World
- Ancient Views on What Is Music
- Contemporary Descriptions of Early Musicians
- Early Views of Music and Ethics
- Early Thoughts on Performance Practice
- Music Performance in Ancient Societies

Renaissance Voices

- Essays on Renaissance Philosophies of Music
- Renaissance Men on Music

www.whitwellbooks.com

www.ingramcontent.com/pod-product-compliance
Lightning Source LLC
Chambersburg PA
CBHW080730300426
44114CB00019B/2543